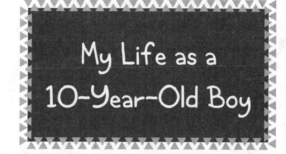

My Life as a
10-Year-Old Boy

NANCY CARTWRIGHT

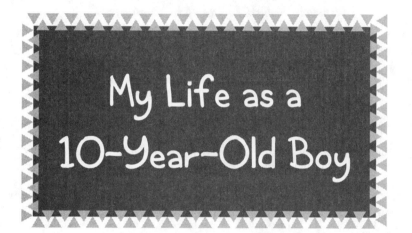

My Life as a
10-Year-Old Boy

✿HYPERION
NEW YORK

Photo credits for sixteen-page photo section:

Pages 1, 2 (top), 4, 6, 7 (top), 8 (bottom), 15: Courtesy of Happy House
Productions
Pages 2 (bottom), 3: Courtesy of the Butler family
Page 5: Courtesy of ABC Photo Archives
Page 7 (bottom): Courtesy of Cypress Point Productions
Page 8 (top): Courtesy of Warner Bros.
Pages 9-14, 16 (top): Courtesy of Mark Kirkland. "The Simpsons"™ and
© 2000 Twentieth Century Fox Film Corporation
Page 16 (bottom): Photo by Angela Swindell. "The Simpsons"™ and ©
2000 Twentieth Century Fox Film Corporation

Printed in the United States of America. For information address:
Hyperion, 77 W. 66th Street,
New York, New York 10023-6298.

Library of Congress Cataloging-in-Publication Data

Cartwright, Nancy.
My life as a ten-year-old boy / Nancy Cartwright.—1st ed.
p.   cm.
ISBN 0-7868-6696-9
1. Simpsons (Television program) 2. Cartwright, Nancy I. Title.
PN1992.77.S58 C37 2000
791.45'72—dc21   00-033433

Book design by Ruth Lee

FIRST EDITION

1 3 5 7 9 10 8 6 4 2

To Daws Butler,
my mentor, my friend—
for opening up his door to me
to let my voice come out.

Contents

• = shorter, celeb-profile–type chapters

Acknowledgments
(In Order of Appearance,
Thank You Very Much)

Bob Killian and Tony Keyes, for believing in a twelve-year-old; Patti McKenny and Doug Anderson, for supporting a "part-time giant"; Leah Funck, for showing us all what it means to have class; Wrecker, for "fried eggs" and *Young Frankenstein*; John Ludlum and JB Bury, for undying passion and compassion; Kathy Umbreit and Nancy Shock, for giving me every opportunity; Anne Schwebel, for giving me your business card; Charles and Myrtis Butler, for your interest and support of me and my family; Susan Cartsonis, for casting me in "One for the Gipper"; Dick Barth, Vic Sutton, Rita Vennari, Mary Ellen Lord, Charles Massey, Libby Westby, Cynthia McLean, Mike Soliday, for twenty years and counting; Joanie Gerber and Frank Welker, for being seasoned pros without any ego; Michael Edwards, for creative casting and brilliant directing; Joanie Schmid, for having to live with me; Staness Jonekos, for your zest and eternal optimism; Susie Glicksman,

Tim Flack and Barbara Corday, for jump-starting my on-camera career; Lynn Stalmaster, for taking a chance on an unknown; Bari Bogart, for submitting me anyway; Jeff Berg, for giving me Fellini's phone number; Camilla Fluxman, for introducing me to Milton; Gary Imhoff, for introducing me to Ron; Murphy, Jack and Lucy, for showing me that I have a whole lot more to learn; Susan Watson, Tom Davis, Jenny Butler and Enid Byrne, for your vigilance and unconditional love; Barry Klein, for checking up on me— constantly; David Royal, for talking that extra fifteen minutes; Steve and Pat Frey, for always being there for me; Lisa Kolpek, for assisting me in reaching heights; Leslie Wells, for coming up with the best title of any book, ever; Francine DeVette, for camouflaging a hole; Sue Bernstein, for your love of artists; Rochelle Goodrich, for your unwavering interest and encouragement; Steve Younger, for doing what you do so well; Susan Royal, for understanding the "Bart" in me and still not giving up; Karen Renna, for really getting me to see the "big picture"; Debbie Damron, for your efficiency, your energy, your charm and just you; Renee Bessone, for your healing hands and loving heart; Samantha Paris, for your unbridled enthusiasm; Jennifer Charm, for making me look beautiful; Angie Swindell, for giving way more than anyone should; Karl Wade, for your willingness "to jump right in"; Carmella Scoggins, for being my new best friend and personal laugh track; Roberta Perry, because you trusted all along; Missy Halperin, Kristen Guertin and Sandie Ceballos, for all your shopping and pampering and unabashed ebullience; Dean Williamson, for going to bat for me; all the great folks at Hyperion, especially Anne Cole, Jodi Glaser-Taub and David Lott, for dealing with the

"Bart" in me; all the great folks at Bloomsbury, for being there first and bringing lots of books; Patrice Monis and Natasha Sasic for the flipbook art that flipped me out; Claudia and Lady, for making my crazy life at home peaceful and clean; Mark Kirkland, for generously contributing his "behind-the-scenes" photos. And finally, although his name truly belongs at the top of the list, Peter Kjenaas, for his unwavering commitment, his sense of integrity and his skill as a professional to really let me be the writer. Only a pro could do something like that. I thank you from the bottom of my Bart-heart.

And if you thought your name should have been here but isn't, keep reading. It is probably in the text of the book. And if it isn't there, call me and I will personally thank you.

Foreword

At the very first *Simpsons* recording session (at that time I don't even think we knew the characters' first names, let alone that they were called the Simpsons), I heard for the first time an amazing facsimile of an actual ten-year-old boy come out of Nancy Cartwright. It was then that I thought, "Boy! L.A.—you can just snap your fingers and, bam, you get the right actor for the right job." I soon discovered how wrong I was, at least about the snapping fingers part. As I did more voice-over work in L.A., I soon discovered there was a small circle of voice-over actors who did the voices of kids (if you exclude child actors), and a *smaller* circle who did it convincingly, and an even *smaller* circle who came up with voices that had a unique personality, and an even *smaller* circle who were funny. Nancy remains in every circle.

To this day I still can't reconcile myself to the fact that Bart Simpson comes out of Nancy Cartwright. Because if you met Nancy—a perky, ever-cheerful, can-do, go-getter of an actress, with a husband and two children—you'd get no indication she could ever play, as Lisa Simpson once called him, a ". . . vile burlesque of irrepressible youth."

Bart Simpson, of course, became the biggest breakout cartoon character since Bugs Bunny and Mickey Mouse. I'm sure I've excluded many favorite and great cartoon characters, but I doubt any have equaled the impact and international recognition that Bart has received. I mean, even the Iraqis think he's a big star!

It is not only Nancy's quick, impeccable comic timing, but also her ability to give depth to what otherwise would be a caricature of a bratty kid. Take a look at the episode "Bart Gets an F." Even after studying hard, Bart still fails his history test. He breaks down and cries—comparing himself to George Washington, who had to surrender Fort Necessity to the French in 1754. Because he expressed his feelings by citing an obscure historical event, his teacher, Mrs. Krabappel, gives him a passing grade. He is so overjoyed, he kisses her and runs out yelling, "I passed! I passed! I . . . kissed the teacher! Ptui!" That scene works so well because of Nancy's ability to switch from emotion to emotion, from moment to moment so quickly and yet convincingly. I remember that as one of the truly touching and poignant moments you can find in a *Simpsons* episode.

Although *The Simpsons* has been blessed with, in my opinion, some of the best writing in television, I think the show is due, in a great part, to the success of Bart Simpson, which in turn is due to Nancy's amazing talent, not only as a voice-over artist, but also as an actress.

Dan Castellaneta

Introduction

I'm Nancy Cartwright.
Who the Hell Are You?!

It is a Saturday morning in 1986. I am in my bed, in my jammies, eating a big bowl of Cap'n Crunch. My dogs are whining because they wish they were on my bed and they love Cap'n Crunch too. But this is "my time" and I don't want to be distracted. After all, three of my favorite shows are on: *Galaxy High, My Little Pony and Friends* and *The Snorks*. Oh, I forgot to mention, they are cartoons. Uh-oh, I doubly forgot to mention, I am in *all* of them. Double uh-oh, I am single. *This* is my life! It didn't occur to me until right now that maybe that was why I was single.

Flash forward, a Sunday evening in 2000. I am in the den with my son on my left and my daughter on my right. Hubby is reaching for the Cap'n Crunch . . . some things never change! The dogs, cats and birds are settled in for the evening. This is "family time" and we don't want to be distracted. After all, *The Simpsons* is on.

A lot has happened in the past fourteen years. The Saturday morning fare has staged a "D-day style" invasion on prime time; and it is no longer referred to as "cartoons" but rather "animation." The styles, the messages and the values have evolved into what I consider a New Golden Age. There is more work for actors and animators than ever thanks to this evolution and I am grateful to be "evolving" right along with it.

I am married and have been for eleven years; I have two kids, Bart and Lisa's age, although not in that order; I am the CEO of my company, Happy House Productions, which produces and develops animated projects for film and television and I am very involved in my community, doing volunteer work for various literacy and drug programs. And, I wonder, does Bart Simpson have anything to do with this?

About five years ago I decided I wanted to write this book. I knew that *The Simpsons* would come to an end some day. (I still don't know when that will be. I just keep imagining me at ninety-six years old, waiting to cross a busy street when some young man approaches me and asks, "May I help you?" and mustering up my best Bart, I say to him, "No way, man!") I decided that I wanted to write it while the show was still on the air. But I felt that I needed to wait. The time did not feel right. Something inside me was telling me that if I just trusted, that the right time would present itself. And that time is now.

Ever since I was Bart's age, voice-overs were what I wanted to do. I remember people telling me that I had a unique voice.

Funny thing is, I also had very short hair, a "pixie" haircut, my mom would call it. There were four of us girls, so short hair was a must. Put that pixie cut with a set of pipes like mine and those same people who thought I had a unique voice also thought I was a boy! The way I see it, I was destined to be Bart.

So, here I was, ten years old. It was holiday time. My parents were terribly clever at Christmas. With six children, they had to economize as much as possible. They were experts at pulling together a theme for that magnificent, wonderful, glorious event and the one year that truly stands out was the "musical instrument Christmas." Cathy got the guitar she had always wanted; Mary Beth already had a piano, but got the metronome that she had her eyes on; Steve triumphed with a trombone; my little brother Poncho's eyes bugged out when he got the set of bongos he had been dreaming about and Marsha, at age seven, scored with a giant-sized, green-haired, Santa-suited troll. (I know it doesn't have anything to do with a musical instrument, but I really loved that troll!)

I hadn't found my booty yet, so when my mom asked, "Hey, Nancy, what is that package tucked way under there?" my heart skipped a beat. It wasn't a very large box, which didn't look good to me. I ravaged the paper and revealed a fourteen-inch-long black case. "A *flute!?* You have got to be kidding me! What a wimpy instrument! There is *no way* I am going to be caught dead playing that thing!" I didn't blurt that out, but I was sure thinking it. Instead, I picked it up and my mom sat there watching me stretch out my fingers, but they juuuuust didn't quiiiiiite reach aaaaaaall the keys. What a bravura performance! She was totally convinced. "Don't worry, honey. I know where Santa does his shopping and he would want you to have a flute that fits, so we'll take it back and get you what you want." Moms are cool.

Little did she know that what I had in mind was nothing like a flute! But when we were standing at the counter of Hauer's Music Store, her jaw dropped about the length of a trombone slide when I blurted out, "I want a trumpet!" I distinctly remember my mother grabbing for the countertop to balance herself. Trumpets were, back then, a "boy toy." She probably was overcome with visions of me hooked on heroin in some New Orleans dive, a bottle of Southern Comfort in one hand and my brass in the other. (Bart would love that life!) The salesclerk patted her on the shoulder and said, "Oh, don't worry, Mrs. Cartwright. Let's just see if she can get a sound out of the mouthpiece. Chances are, it won't happen. It takes quite a bit of lip to get the right sound." He handed me the mouthpiece and I blurted out a riff that would have made Louis Armstrong proud! I showed Joe Salesman who had "quite a bit of lip"!

Year number ten was a big one in this girl's life. Being the only girl trumpet player in the band wasn't enough. An upcoming schoolwide speech contest was announced. If you were the winner in your class you would move on to compete against the entire grade. All I needed was to find a story, memorize it, say it for my class and win. That didn't sound too difficult. My folks had invested in a set of Childcraft Books put out by World Book encyclopedia. I started going through it, trying to find the "ideal" story to tell. I couldn't decide between "Little Toot" and "The Three Billy Goats Gruff." It was my mom who pulled me through the dilemma. She told me to take a look at Rudyard Kipling's "How the Camel Got His Hump." She suggested it would be better since it wasn't one of the "old standards." I read it and it totally quenched my thirst. I told her, "You're right, Mom! This is a story that deserves to be told!" I took it on as my personal mission.

I edited the story down to a solid ten-minute piece, complete with transitions. I worked on it and perfected it, practically driving the rest of the family nuts saying my lines over and over. The best part of the speech was when the camel said, "Hrrrumph!" The line isn't particularly funny, but when I said it, I threw my head back and hrrrumph'd it forward, throwing my whole body into it. You couldn't help but laugh, if only for the fact that I looked so completely silly.

Competing against the members of my own class wasn't so difficult. There were only two other girls and one of them was so nervous, she threw up and was disqualified. The other one recited the poem "The Whisperer," but nobody could hear what she was saying. This is not to say that I won by default. I didn't. I just don't remember any other competitors.

Being the winner for my class now meant that I was pitted against the winners of all the fourth-grade classes. There were four of us in that final round. I don't remember much about the kids before me. I was pretty nervous. I was assigned to go last, so I had to sit through all the other speeches, listening to the laughter and the applause. The entire school was in attendance. Part of me thinks that I won because I was such a petite little gal. I wasn't even four feet tall. I think I actually "squeaked" when I walked. But, when my shining moment of "hrrrumph" came, I milked it for all it was worth and walked away with First Place.

The summers between fourth grade and high school were filled with lots of fun, games and especially, children's theater. At the ripe old age of twelve, I was invited to be the youngest member of SYTCo—the Summer Youth Theater Company. Mostly comprised of high school students, we traveled around Ohio entertaining the public with original musicals *at no charge.* From playing a "part-time giant" to an American Indian from the Ocheerunamuck tribe to marching around as Lt. Potshot, a toy soldier, I had a blast creating some wonderful parts. Ironically, they were all boys! It was with this group that not only did I learn to say the alphabet *backward,* but I also learned how to drip like a faucet, sound like a cement mixer and do a man-trapped-in-a-barrel—a very visual sound effect. This was my early training for what I would later be paid for!

I was very active in all sorts of extracurricular activities. I was captain of the gymnastics team, lead in the junior class play and active in our community theater. I also asked plenty of guys out . . . they didn't always say yes, but I wasn't going to sit and wait for the phone to ring. I worked at Friendly's Ice Cream and played the horn with the Fairmont West marching band. We touted the fact that we were one of the only "all brass" bands in the state of Ohio. There were about one hundred of us, which is quite a powerful sound, as you might imagine. The kids who normally played woodwind instruments in the concert band had to learn how to play a brass instrument during the football season. I thought that was remarkable. And we Dragons really pulled it off.

By my senior year I was well-established as a "go-getter" and took particular pride in wearing the extra epaulette on my uniform that indicated I was a squad leader. My squad consisted of myself and three other horn players who relied on me to yell out the various directions during the halftime show program. This was a show not to miss . . . if only for the fact that I actually yelled the commands so loudly that you could hear me from the bleachers!

David Robert Finkham was the band director and, boy, did I give him a hard time! I had a penchant for talking (duh!) and one time, immediately following the local "Holiday at Home" parade held on Labor Day, someone in the crowd got my attention so I sat my horn down right in the middle of the street and went to talk to him. Big mistake. The rest of the band eventually disbanded. Finally I realized that everyone had gone and that I didn't have my horn. I headed back to the spot where we had finished off and just as I was about to step off the curb, a truck rolled by, smashing my horn into a pancake. Ouch. Poor Mr. Finkham. I have no doubt that when I graduated, he took a long-deserved vacation. In the meantime, he had to deal with yours truly.

We would get our music on Mondays, along with our guide sheets for the formations that we were to do for the show. That afternoon we would begin to put it all together. The hours were long, but it was never boring, especially when the squad leader, thankyouverymuch, didn't quite know a "fancy-to-the-rear" was nothing remotely similar to an "about face."

The high school was about a half mile from the football stadium. Every Friday night it was part of the ritual to meet at the school parking lot, in full-dress uniform, and march in formation to the stadium. We would play the school song about ten times and intersperse it with songs we had learned for previous halftime shows. This was one of the highlights of being in the band because, all along the way, the neighbors who lived between the school and the stadium would go out on their lawns and cheer us as we marched to the game. This was at least as fun as the halftime show itself. We *rocked*!

The drum squad kept the whole thing going, beating out the cadence that we would respond to: da da da-da da. And we would answer, "D.R.F." in homage to Mr. Finkham. And this would go on and on until we reached the stadium. Shortly into my senior year, the chant changed a bit. The cadence was still the same but the response was amended: da da da-da da . . . "Eat my shorts!" I don't know who came up with it, but that drum squad and a couple of "trouble-making trumpet players" were responsible for nearly every minute we ended up standing at attention for disrupting the whole band! Regardless, Mr. Finkham's initials were never mentioned again, and the history of one of the most successful phrases ever to be printed on a T-shirt was established.

Sad but true, I was not destined to be a trumpet player, ambulant or not. My heart lay elsewhere—specifically in Room 316, South Unit, Mr. Kuldau's speech class. Mr. K, as we all called him, was one of those teachers who you never forget. He was one of those teachers you wish your children would have been taught by because he cared so much. A lot of the other teachers would roll their eyes when Mr. K would canter down the hall. I believe they wished their students adored them as much as his students adored Mr. K. He was the one who inspired me to take this unique-sounding voice and put it to some use.

I quickly immersed myself in speech. I just loved it. Forensics had two programs. One was public speaking and, in particular, debate. I was not a debater. I left that to the future attorneys and politicians. The other aspect was called Individual Events. We'd prepare speeches in a number of categories, including humorous and dramatic interpretation, expository, prose, poetry and dramatic duo. I was a kid in a candy shop. I was exposed to some of the best literature out there, from Shakespeare to Neil Simon. Mr. K recommended "Many Moons," a children's story by James Thurber. It still is one of my favorites.

I worked on this story, cutting it into a ten-minute presentation. We never had to memorize, although I always did because in telling the story in competition I aways wanted to look at the audience, connect with them. I felt this was the key, and that is something that I still believe today. It is all about "connecting."

In a tournament, you were assigned to a round with about four or five others in the same category. There might have been a total of thirty people competing in any one category. You'd do three preliminary rounds, a semifinal round and then a final round. You would be judged on delivery, creativity and choice of material. It was a terrific confidence builder and also an activity that parents supported wholeheartedly—no equipment to buy, no uniform to hate and no physical to suffer through. It was an ideal extracurricular "sport."

We were a unified group, we were. Getting up at four in the morning on a Saturday to haul our tired butts to the school in order to ride a school bus three hours to Urbana in the freezing-cold, frostbite-inducing winters of Ohio. *We loved it!*

That first year I really scored with "Many Moons," having

created six or seven quirky and original characters. My brothers were bringing home the Little League and Soapbox Derby trophies, while I was placing first in Humorous Interpretation and had the "hardware" to prove it.

The next year, I did even better with Thurber's "Thirteen Clocks," creating even more characters, I think about a dozen in all. The coolest thing about this kind of activity is that it gives you permission to do all the things that you aren't supposed to be doing: acting silly, creating weird-sounding voices, contorting your face to become different characters. It was all in the spirit of play. My training ground. I am sure that Bart was in there somewhere.

When I would get my critiques back from the judges, there was one consistent note: "You should do cartoon voices." There seemed to be an awful lot of agreement on this point. And that was when I decided that that was what I wanted to do.

I ended up placing first in the National District Tournament for two years in a row. This had never been done before and I was awarded with a scholarship from the host of the competition, Ohio University. This was my ticket out of this nightmare! (Kidding. Just seeing if you were paying attention.)

At Ohio U I was to compete on their speech team, doing pretty much what I had done before, but now, instead of just competing in the high school district, I would be traveling to different universities in different states. Being on the speech team while attending college was not unlike getting paid for being on *The Simpsons*: I was doing what I loved and not only getting credit for competing, but getting to travel and meet people, win cool trophies and have some pretty wild parties . . . and all on the university's dime!

The summer of 1977, I had landed myself a terrific part-time job at WING radio station. Get it? Dayton, Ohio. W-I-N-G? Home of the Wright Brothers. "Wingin' it in Dayton!"

For years, the station was located downtown. In 1946, Jonathan Winters, genius comedian, improv artist, writer and fellow Daytonian, was their morning deejay. He used to pull some real stunts, as you can imagine. Jim Bennett, a young local, tried to read the news but would constantly crack up because of Jonathan's antics. He went so far as to roll a bowling ball at Jim while he was on the air! Jim eventually became the president and general manager of WING. He later moved the station ten miles south to Kettering, my hometown.

Looking out the kitchen window into our backyard, I could see the backside of the radio station. Cutting across the field that separated us took five minutes, if you ran half the way. That field was our playground when I was a kid. It was an incredible field of tall grass and flowering weeds that went on and on forever until it met up with a small wooded area. Depending on the time of year, the field would become a baseball diamond or a football field or a volleyball court. And, in the winter, we would grab our sleds and head to those woods because it had a nice steady slope, perfect for a downhill toboggan race. Because of its versatility, about sixty-five kids in the neighborhood just about lived in that field.

I would be heading off for my second year at Ohio University that fall and I was earning a little extra cash by filling in for radio station employees who went on vacation. By the end of summer I had learned many aspects of the radio business: reception, accounting, scheduling, promotions. But I lived for the four-minute segment that I actually got to be on the air.

Every afternoon at 4:45 and 5:45 I would join the deejay in the booth for the drive-time show, "The Poolside Show with Ken Warren." Kenny and I hit it off right from the start. Weatherman Bob Breck worked across town at a local TV station and we would patch him in as if he were right there with us for a "poolside" show. Ken would put on sound effects of people diving into a pool, splashing around and gaily drinking martinis. It was pretty silly. I became the unofficial "lifeguard" of the pool, Lily Padd. She was a distant "cousin" of Bart. Ken kept having me on.

Most of the folks from the station knew of my passion—especially Jim, Ken and the morning deejay, Steve Kirk. "Kirkie" was a master. This guy was so quick and so improvisational, I began to realize what it really takes to be a voice-artist. He would have Lily Padd on occasionally, but mostly, this guy *ruled* and showed us all the way it should be done.

They really supported my dreams. I would sneak up to the station at night and work on putting together a tape of all my characterizations. It is a must in the voice-over industry to have a demo tape of the characters and styles you do. Typically, a demo tape is two and a half to three minutes long. I did not know this. My first demo was no less than thirteen minutes!

Not long into the summer, a gal from Warner Bros. Records came into the station to promote their music. Jim introduced us, thinking that because she was from Warner Bros. she might know someone who could help me break into animation. To him (and to me, for that matter) Warner Bros. meant Mel Blanc. This might be just the ticket. I shook hands with Anne Schwebel and we chatted a bit. She gave me her card and said that if I wrote to her she would get my letter to someone in the animation department, as she didn't know much about it herself.

Anne was good to her word. She sent me a letter listing the names of several contacts in the industry. I didn't recognize most of them, but I sent out my demo tape with cover letter anyway. The last name on the list had no address, just a phone number. But this one stood out the most—Daws Butler. He was the voice of most of the characters that I grew up with: Huckleberry Hound, Yogi Bear, Quick-Draw McGraw, Baba-Looey, Elroy, Cogswell, Lambsy, Chilly Willy, Augie Doggie, Henry Orbit, Hokey Wolf, Blabber Mouse, Super Snooper, Lippy the Lion, Wally Gator, Peter Potamus, Capt. Skyhook and Cap'n Crunch. (It was that last one that really locked me in!) I was a fast fan!

I thought, "What the heck. I'm gonna call him." So I went into our basement and gave him a ring. On the other end of the line, an answering machine picked up. This was the summer of '77. They didn't have answering machines in Ohio yet. I listened to his outgoing message (with a British accent): "Hello. My name is Percival Pickles. I'm Mr. Butler's butler. Mr. Butler is not home just now. If you would like to leave a message, wait for the beep. (Long pause) *Beep.*" And that was it. I was stunned. I didn't know how to respond. This was the coolest thing I had ever heard. I quickly gathered my thoughts and left my message (in a Cockney accent): " 'ello Mr. Butler. This is Nancy Cartwright. I am from

Kettering, O'io. I understand that you teach voice-acting classes and I am very interested in this. Please write to me at 788 Lovetta Drive, Kettering, O'io, 45429. Thank you and pip-pip cheerio!"

With that, I hung up the phone. I couldn't believe that I had done that! I thought, he is going to think I am crazy, calling all the way from Ohio. . . . Then I realized, as long as he thinks I am crazy, I should call him back and get him to call me. I don't want to wait for a letter! So I called him again (same Cockney): "Mr. Butler, instead of writing me, why don't you just give me a ring-a-ding on the ol' telly? My number is 513-555-7009. Call me and we can have a chat. Oh, call collect. Tootles."

I didn't have to wait that long. Next thing I knew, the phone rang and I scrambled to get it. On the other end of the line was Daws. "Hollywood calling. Will you accept the charges?" *Omygod!* It was him!

He became my fast friend. He agreed to send me a bunch of scripts in the mail if I would send him my demo tape. And this was the beginning of our student-mentor relationship. He would send me one of his original scripts in the mail and I would take a portable tape recorder and lay it down. I would then send it back to him and he would listen and critique it. He'd send me the notes along with another script. He was absolutely amazing. Always encouraging. Always positive.

In one letter, he wrote, "Dear little sweet protégée, Nancy! The years are going to start going faster now . . . no doubt about that—and for a girl a lot has to happen between nineteen and twenty-five. The main thing is not to get involved in some of the traps that are put out for your young years—the beauty schools, modeling schools—talent schools. Most of them are pure hokum. I'm not hokum, tho'—and I'm old enough to be pure." And he signed it, "Take care—and don't be cosmetic unless you're going out on a Saturday night. Your well-meaning mentor, Daws." Sweet.

That fall I was off to Ohio U for my sophomore year. I had received another scholarship and was back in competition again. By now, I was receiving packages from Daws about once every two to three weeks. Usually the scripts were just monologues, but occasionally Daws would send me a script that was a dialogue between a man and a woman or two women. I started asking some of the other team members to be a part of the tapes I was sending to Daws. They eagerly joined me and were interested in what was developing with me and "Yogi."

That year, Ohio U made it to the National Speech Tournament held at Monmouth College in New Jersey. Schools from all over the country were represented. The competition was grueling. Three days of preliminary rounds, then semifinals, quarterfinals, and finally, finals!

By this time I already knew that I was not going to be returning to Ohio U. I wasn't quite sure where I was going to go instead—have you ever heard of a major in "Cartoon-voices"? All I knew was that I wanted to go out with a bang! I competed in five different categories: humorous, after-dinner, dramatic interp, poetry and exposition. It was with this last speech that I made it into the final round. In fact, there was only one other Ohio U student who made it into the final round. He was a year older than I, a little more experienced in this arena. He took me aside, thinking he was going to be giving this underclassman a pep talk. With all the intensity of a future lawyer or stand-up comedian, he said, "We *are* OU. We are all that's left." And he looked at me and I was more calm than he was. I walked away with fifth in the nation on my speech, "The Art of Animation."

I was determined to pursue this dream of doing cartoons. I knew from the beginning what I wanted and how I was going to get it. No one could sway me. Nothing could get in my way—or so I thought.

THE name Nancy Cartwright almost never became associated with *The Simpsons*. My name wouldn't have appeared on any of the multiple animated shows I came to voice and some other lucky girl would be writing this book.

My plan almost came up short when my dad, Frank, was driving me back home, at the end of my sophomore year, from my final quarter at Ohio U. I was about to transfer to UCLA, to work with Daws, face-to-face. Suddenly he interrupted my visions of grandeur in the Far West. "Well, kiddo," he said in a tone that was at once cute and also somehow strong. "Now that you completed all your tests and got another year behind you, I have some bad news. Your mother—"

My heart skipped a beat. "Is she okay?"

"Let's just say that she is . . . more comfortable. She's in the hospital again."

FLASHBACK to six months before: Mom and I are doing sit-ups in the den, hooking our feet under the couch. (I've always considered this cheating because when you hook your feet under something, you aren't really using your stomach. But I had acquiesced for Mom's sake.)

We are crunching to the BeeGees' "Stayin' Alive." ". . . and five, and six, and seven, and . . . Mom, you didn't even do seven! Come on!"

"I know," she says, totally supine, her breath sounding ragged and desperate. "It feels like there's ground-up glass in my stomach." The next day she was in Kettering Hospital.

MIRACULOUSLY, she made it home from the "visit" at the end of my sophomore year at Ohio U, after the doctors had successfully removed yet another tumor. And she was actually feeling pretty darn good. We got down to planning "our" trip once again. I would read my letters to Daws out loud before I sent them and she would smile and give me a tip or two. "Tell him about your dreams, Nancy." But there were no more sit-ups, no more mention of her "getting back in shape."

She tried so hard to hide the effects of the invisible growth inside, the growth that was eating her up. Within two weeks even she couldn't cover the telltale signs. She reached over one evening to adjust my hair as I read yet another book on "making it" in Hollywood, and I looked up in time to see a spasm of pain cross her face. The next day, she made her last trip to the hospital.

I would have totally given up California, Daws, voice-overs and my future plans, if I could just have my mom! I looked at my plane ticket, my ticket out, and knew that I would stay there in Ohio and never leave. I would become a mom like her, exactly like her, a woman I could only aspire to be, and it would have been a good life too.

In her last couple days she refused to see me while she visited with each member of my family. I was devastated until I got word that she wanted to see me. I had no idea what to expect and didn't know what I was going to say.

When I stepped in her room, the transformation in her condition was terrifying. It was as if she were already more than half gone. I sat next to her and held her soft hands. They were unbelievably soft, almost like a baby's. I just sat there and tried not to cry, unsuccessfully. She asked me if I had all my bags packed and did I go shopping and buy a couple new outfits and did I decide what I was going to wear when I met Daws in person. Still being "The Mom." By the end of the conversation, her eyes were getting heavy and she looked so beautiful and soft. I remember kissing her good-bye and telling her I loved her. That was the last conversation she had with anyone. We got a call at three in the morning that my mother had passed away.

On September 19, 1978, my dad and I flew joylessly to California. And thus began a whole new chapter in my life.

UCLA was everything and more than I expected it to be. A little paradise located in Westwood, neighboring on Beverly Hills, Hollywood and Santa Monica, it was like no school I had ever imagined.

I had called Daws and told him that I was all settled in at Sproul Hall, one of the dorms on campus. He invited my dad and me out to lunch that day. I was so curious about where he lived, Beverly Hills and all. I pictured some three-story mansion with guard dogs protecting the property. I wondered who we might see watering the lawn, who were his neighbors?

We found his house and it wasn't anything at all what I expected. It was a very comfortable, modest three-bedroom Spanish-style hacienda. Charming and very comfortable for the Butler family. The garage had been converted into Daws's studio and also had a guest apartment upstairs.

Daws answered the door. There he stood, all four feet, ten inches of him. He smiled from ear to ear and said, "Don't just stand there. Give your old mentor a hug!" What a sweetie.

My dad left me in good hands. He went back to Ohio and I carried on with my new life.

There was no speech team at UCLA, but there was plenty of theater. I found that in this time of extreme depression and loss, the best thing I could do was immerse myself in doing the things I loved. It saved my life.

On Sundays, I would catch the number 86 bus into Beverly Hills to work with Daws. He and I were to do a one-hour lesson, working with his own material—reading, changing, adjusting, working with the microphone, editing—just having a great time. His class wasn't just about technique. He would focus on all phases of acting, expression and communication. He was the first to get me to realize that voice-overs weren't any less demanding than acting. It took all the emotion and especially the commitment to the character in order to communicate what that character was feeling. He believed that "Talent cannot be taught. It must exist. But if it does exist at all, it can be nurtured and expanded." So, the hour-long lesson was never an hour. It always expanded into no less than four.

Daws and I would just lose ourselves in that studio. He would show me old film clips of characters that he had voiced, including the bunny from the Bosco spots: "Chocolate tastes like Bosco." There was a whole series of National Bohemian Beer spots. He also voiced for Snowdrift cooking shortening, which is now called Crisco. He did tons of Kellogg's spots, before Snap, Crackle and Pop. It was fascinating seeing the animation of that time. Some of it was superb—technically, they weren't as advanced. They were just simple clean spots; and they didn't have to cut corners, like so many of them do today, for budgetary reasons.

After a pretty full afternoon, Daws and his lovely wife, Myrtis, would take me out to Love's BBQ Pit on Pico near Doheny before taking me back to the dorm. They would tell me stories like how Huckleberry Hound was characterized after a neighbor of Myrtis's when Daws was courting her. "Weeeeeeeell, ... hiiiiiiiiiii theeeeeeeere Daaaaaaaaaaaws. Hooooooooow aaaaaaaaaare yooooooooou doooooooin?" By the time he got done sayin' "hi," it was time to get Myrtis home!

Time moved quickly because I was keeping really busy. Another new friend had "adopted" me and I would spend the holidays at her family's house in Huntington Beach. Colleen and I became "buds" and she inspired the "Bart" in me.

We were taking a set construction class together. Mostly we were "grunts," doing a lot of busy work and, in particular, painting the set for Chekhov's *Three Sisters*. It was a lot of manual labor and a lot of brown paint. We would meet in the shop behind the main stage theater, fill our buckets with brown paint and just keep painting flat after flat with this brown goopy stuff. We kept teasing the teacher's assistant by threatening to eat the paint because it looked so much like chocolate pudding. By the end of the class period, we always had more paint on us than on the flats because neither of us ever quite mastered the technique—but we had the most fun. We were really silly girls and the teacher's assistant for the class seemed to get a kick out of our antics.

The night before the last class, I told Colleen, "Let's really get Leslie. But we need to go shopping." So off we went and bought ourselves a brand-new paint bucket, a couple of wide brushes and fifteen "four-packs" of chocolate pudding.

The next morning, we filled the bucket with the pudding and, when Leslie came into the shop, we greeted her licking the brushes, with chocolate pudding on our faces, and said, "Mmmm, pudding!" Leslie about bust a gut.

If Chekhov only knew . . . it would have been *Three Sisters—and Bart.*

Around that same time, Daws and I had been working very closely together on my first "professional" demo tape. It was exactly two and a half minutes long! He and I laid down about eight to ten readings of different characters in different situations. He guided me to a facility where they made duplicates of the recordings and I designed a label for them. At that time, the demos were done on reel-to-reels. Over the years, the demos have gone from reels to cassettes to CDs and nowadays, even DVDs. Having worked with tape has a tendency to make one feel very "experienced" when there are kids in the business in their early twenties who have never even *seen* a reel-to-reel tape recorder. Good grief!

Once my tape was complete, I was ready to go to Hanna-

Barbera with Daws. He wanted to "show me off" and give me a real firsthand look at how a recording session goes. So off we went, demos in hand, to a taping of *The All-New Popeye Hour*. This was the first highlight of my career.

To be in the same room with all these people who I had heard so much about was the first of many highlights. Their names were familiar because Daws had talked about them so much: Frank Nelson, Julie Bennett, Joanie Gerber, Don Messick, Patty Parris, William Schallert, Hal Smith, John Stephenson, Jean VanderPyle and the incomparable Frank Welker. I was in voice-over heaven.

Daws was the voice of Wimpy and I just sat there, mesmerized. I watched and listened. It was everything I could do to keep from jumping up and participating.

After the session, Daws introduced me to everyone and totally embarrassed me by telling them that I was from Ohio and I had moved out to California to study with him while going to UCLA. I shook a bunch of hands and smiled a lot. Then he introduced me to about five of the directors that worked there. But the one director who time and time again proved to be incredibly loyal and shortly thereafter brought me back for my first audition was Gordon Hunt.

Gordon was originally the casting director at the Mark Taper Forum, one of America's top regional theaters located in Los Angeles. He has taught and directed professional theater for many years. Gordon has directed hundreds of hours of animation in addition to over fifty hours of sitcoms. He has earned three DramaLogue Awards for his work in theater and a Directors Guild of America award for *Mad About You*. At the time, I had no idea that meeting this man would catapult my career into the arena that I so passionately desired access to.

Within one month, Gordon called me and arranged for me to audition for a new animated show they were doing called *Richie Rich*. The only problem was that I didn't have a car and didn't know how to get there and couldn't afford a cab. No problem—Daws to the rescue!

I was escorted back to the studio and met Gordon's assistant, Ginny McSwain. She helped set me up and made me feel very comfortable. Everyone was so incredibly helpful. I had the oddest feeling . . . Actually, it was odd only because it *wasn't* odd: It was as if I had been there and done this before. I felt totally at home and comfortable. I wasn't nervous at all. I just read the part of Gloria, Richie Rich's girlfriend, thanked everyone and said goodbye.

Within a week, I got a call at my dorm from Ginny saying that I got the part. I couldn't believe it! My first professional job! I was a working actress and I didn't even have an agent.

Gordon and Ginny proved to be incredibly loyal fans. They would continue to have me in to read part after part. And I worked, job after job for Hanna-Barbera. The work was fast and fun. This was outstanding! And when the residual checks started to come, I really loved what I was doing! I was still in school and making my living as an artist.

Because of the no-car situation, I was in desperate need of some wheels. I got myself a local newspaper that advertised used cars and came across a 1968 Opel Kadette. It looked like a smashed potato—I was in love. I bought it for $350 and named it Spud. This got me to my auditions and jobs . . . barely. Poor Spud got up to 45 mph if you floored it. I made up a bumper sticker that read, "It's floored," so the people passing me on the 405 and giving me the finger would understand.

Fall quarter, 1980, I had the opportunity to reprise a character that I had done in a play at UCLA the spring before. I was playing the part of a twelve-year-old girl and seeing how I was a senior in college, the casting was a bit creative.

Opening weekend I got a call from an agency saying that they wanted to meet with me. So, on a whim, I thought, Cool. Maybe I can do a little on-camera work to supplement my voice-over career. (FYI—for *most* actors, this is usually done the other way 'round. But it didn't matter to me—it was all good fun.)

Next thing I knew, I had signed with the agency and was immediately sent out for a "general." This is when you take a general meeting with a casting director, not necessarily for a particular part in a project, but more to just meet and find out about each other. I was warned that I might be asked to do a "cold reading," which means no rehearsal, but this was totally fine by me because of all my work with Daws and my forensics training.

Sure enough, we met and I read for a character in a sitcom called *In Trouble*. The character I read was one of the leads. Next thing I know I am being escorted into a room where twelve network executives had gathered to hear me read. I didn't know what was going on and had no idea that this "reading" was really an "acting" and was going to determine the future of my on-camera career. Turns out they loved it and gave me more money for one week of work than most people made in a whole year! The pilot was forgettable but it jump-started my on-camera career. And, for the first time, I got to write my dad a check!

That summer my agent called and asked if I would be interested in working with an improv troupe back in Ohio . . . with Jonathan Winters. *Omygod, are you kidding me?* Where do I go? What do I do?

I showed up at the audition at the Zephyr Theater on Melrose. It was jam-packed with actors and the line went all the way down the street. Jeez, you get the idea that actors want to act or something.

After what seemed longer than anyone should have to wait for anything so ethereal, I was escorted in. Jonathan was sitting center stage, finishing up a bit with one of his millions of characters.

"Hi, Jonathan. My name's Nancy Cartwright. I am from Dayton, Ohio, and we both worked at WING. Jim Bennett was my boss and man, does he have stories about you!"

I was hired on the spot. I am not sure if he knew whether I had "stuff" on him or not—which I don't, unless you consider that Jim told me this great story about how Jonathan once got a horse up three flights of stairs and into the radio station to be the "surprise guest"! What a hoot.

I went back with a troupe of actors and we performed for two weeks at Kenyon College, Jonathan's alma mater. What was way cool about this gig, of course, were the rehearsals and the perfomances. Jonathan is such an extraordinary "mad genius." His perfection of tapping into "characters of the mind" and then utilizing them for his art is unsurpassed. Later, when he was working with Robin Williams, it was so evident that Robin and Jonathan were artistic soul mates. Back at Kenyon College, it was all we could do to keep up with him. We had very loosely worked out a number of improv sketches, but with Jonathan, you just never know. The shows were hilarious and we got rave reviews. And my family got to see me work with the best of the best— another highlight in my career.

Once back in Los Angeles, I got an audition for the lead in a movie-of-the-week, called *Marian Rose White*. Apparently, casting had been going on for some time and no one was right for the part. I got the script and found out that the title character, Marian, was very childlike and did some crazy things. Her sense of humor was mistaken for being a little crazy, and that she had bad eyesight and wore Coke-bottle glasses didn't help the situation. So I showed up at the audition with a foam lobster visor that Jonathan had given me. I had also bought these glasses that made my eyes look as big as the frames. I studied my part and sat in the lobby, waiting to meet the producers. Prior to going in, though, I reconsidered what I was going to do. I changed my mind and stashed the glasses under the chair, along with the lobster hat. Later on, after I had been given the part, I was told that they saw me sitting in the lobby with the hat and glasses on and it was right then that they agreed, As long as she can read, she has the part.

Shortly after *Marian*, I went in to meet Joe Dante (*Gremlins, Innerspace, The 'Burbs* and *Small Soldiers*). He was just about to start work on *Twilight Zone: The Movie*. I was reading for the part of Ethyl, the girl who gets eaten by the animated wolf. Joe was/is a total cartoon buff, and once he took a look at my resumé and noticed Daws Butler's name on it, we were off and running, sharing anecdotes about Daws and animation. After about twenty minutes, he said, "Considering your background, I don't see how I could cast anybody *but* you in this part!" And that was that.

Meanwhile, I was juggling this new on-camera career with more work in voice-overs. I continued to work on one show after another. Ginny McSwain eventually branched out on her own and is a legend in her own right in the animation industry, having logged in some 2,500 shows. It is not unusual for her to be working on four or five at a time. She is a joy to work with—utterly irreverent, delightfully acerbic, witty, charming and smart. I *love* being bossed around by her! She has since become a good friend and business associate and has always been very loyal—a quality that is rare in this highly competitive business.

Another loyal supporter who encouraged my talent was Andrea Romano, who was Ginny's replacement at Hanna-Barbera. She eventually headed up casting at Warner Bros., where I worked with her on *Animaniacs* and *Pinky and the Brain*. She is another artist who takes great care with the cast she chooses—always dedicated to those she knows can "deliver the goods," and yet always willing to give "the new kid" a chance. She has just the right measure of professionalism to keep raising the bar for talent and the right measure of playfulness to help an actor make it over. Between the two of them, I made quite a nice living doing voice-over work.

I worked at various studios doing *Shoots & Ladders, Glo-Friends, Moondreamers, Pound Puppies, Young Astronauts, The Chipmunk Adventure, Dink the Little Dinosaur, The Pink Pan-*

ther, Rugrats, Popeye and Son, Monchichi's, Fantastic Max, Goof Troop, Problem Child and *Space Ace.*

Once I had graduated from UCLA, I decided that as long as I was an actress, I was going to find related work in the industry. There were plenty of opportunities. And fortunately I am just pushy enough to find and get myself in touch with those who can provide such opportunities. One very cool job I had was being a part of a "loop group." *Looping* is the technique that was used before digital sound came along, but the groups of actors who are hired to do replacement dialogue are still called loop groups. The digital technique they employ now is called ADR, which stands for "automated dialogue replacement." ADR is a technique that allows actors to replace or enhance the voice-track in a motion picture or animated project. You see, when a film is shot, the only dialogue being recorded is that of characters in the scene who have written lines. All the other characters provide "background" and are played by extras, hopefully under a union contract. Imagine a scene taking place in a restaurant and Tom Hanks and Meg Ryan are doing all the talking. Without a loop group adding the "atmosphere," all the other sounds you'd hear in the restaurant, it might seem more like a library or perhaps, a funeral parlor, which would be a little odd, especially if Tom and Meg were eating. I was fortunate that I got involved in a couple of "loop groups" that specialized in ADR. I did tons of "background" characters for mostly live-action films. This is a terrific training ground for an actor because it challenges your improvisation skills. Of course that new sound track is turned down so low that you will never catch any of the dialogue of my performances, but that is just the idea. The job is merely to enhance the scene, make it more real.

Mickie McGowan has one of the best loop groups, appropriately named "Lip Shtick," and I will be forever grateful to her. She brought me in as one of the voice-over talents on such projects as *Clan of the Cave Bear, Silverado, Sixteen Candles, Back to the Future 2* and *The Color Purple*. In *Who Framed Roger Rabbit* I was the shoe that got "dipped." Never having been dipped in acid before, it took a certain amount of improv to conjure up the emotion of what it must feel like to be slowly and precisely dipped into a gurgling vat of green oozing acid. As this was my first off-screen death scene, the performance garnered me a round of applause from my peers. (By the way, some of the best acting is done on stage in an acting class or on a soundstage with a dozen or so of your contemporaries. Kudos to all of those unacknowledged performances.)

With a couple more movies-of-the-week and a quick jaunt to Spain to work with Jennifer Jason Leigh in Paul Verhoeven's *Flesh and Blood*, I got a call to audition for *Cheers*. At the end of the audition piece, my character turns and says one more line before exiting the bar, and I couldn't resist. With a roomful of producers, assistants, casting directors and writers, I turned, said my line and walked right out the door. That in itself wasn't so surprising, but the fact that I just kept on going totally threw everyone for a loop. By the time I got home, my phone was ringing and I was cast as the part of Cynthia, the girlfriend of Andy Andy, who was trying to murder Diane.

I come from the school of thought that you can never stop learning. UCLA was a wonderful training ground for me, allowing me to master all the technical aspects of theater—lighting, costuming, set design, etc.—but the area of acting needs to be addressed constantly, even after graduation. I asked some friends what acting class they would recommend. The name Milton Katselas/Beverly Hills Playhouse kept coming up, so I checked it out. Very soon I found myself in one of the most professional, top-rated classes in town. I was having the time of my life finding out more about the actresses I loved and admired: Fanny Brice, Judy Holliday and especially Fellini's own Giulietta Masina. I was working on scenes from some of their best works, including *Funny Girl, Born Yesterday* and *La Strada*. It was with this last one that I embarked on a journey that would change the focus of my career.

With a strong recommendation from Milton, I began to research and study Giulietta Masina's work in *La Strada*. This is a classic piece of art and, if you are unfamiliar with it, you should definitely check it out.

I began to put up every imaginable scene from it in my acting class. It was an incredibly creative time in my career because I got to cast the other parts and work with so many different actors, all in the effort to bring Gelsomina, Masina's character in the film, to life. Finally, after no less than half a dozen scenes, I decided that I wanted to get the rights to produce *La Strada* as a legitimate stage production. Now, this is no small undertaking, as I was about to find out.

I want to preface this by saying that at this time in my career I was clearly looking for something. I was quite content doing tons of voice-overs. I was in the top two percent of the Screen Actors Guild, making a living by acting in the profession. I was doing what it was I had set out to do and doing it big time. But, with all that said, *I still wanted more!* I wanted to shake up my life, invite a little challenge. And a trip to Italy was just the right ticket.

I tried for months to get the stage rights to produce this play, but kept running into all sorts of brick walls. I wrote to Fellini. No answer. I wrote letters to the producers, Dino De Laurentiis and Carlo Ponti. To no avail. I wrote another letter to Fellini. Not home. I was beginning to feel a little frustrated. I said to myself, "Forget trying to get the rights. Go to Italy to meet Fellini in person! I'll find him. He'll meet me and fall in love with me. He will see what a great artist I am and will beg me to do *La Strada* on stage. I don't just owe it to myself, but I owe it to Fellini and all his fans throughout the universe. This isn't just a trip, it is a personal mission. I not only shall go, *I must* go!"

And so the journey began. I had just completed a wonderful play at the Skylight Theatre and met a gal who told me she wanted to go to Italy too. I thought this would be great—a couple of chicks traveling all over Italy. What fun! We began Italian lessons immediately. Verbal self-defense would be our best tool. "Vada via che sa di aglio." *Buzz off, garlic breath.* "Non mi tocchi." *Don't touch me.* "Fa schifo." *You're disgusting.* I figured these might come in handy.

It was the night before the trip. I had just sat on my suitcase to lock the damn thing when the phone rang. It was my traveling companion. "What?! You can't go?! Why not? Uh huh . . . uh huh. You mean to tell me that you didn't tell your agent that you are going and now you have an audition tomorrow?! You have got to be kidding me. Uh huh. You're not . . . Well, okay. Ciao, bella." Bereft but undaunted, I was flying solo.

So that was it. My bags were packed, I had my *How to Flirt Your Way Through Italy Handbook* as quoted earlier and enough magazines and other reading material to take me to Rome and back. However, once I arrived in Milan and my luggage went on to Frankfurt, Germany, I realized that this was not going to be just any ordinary trip. I met some of the most bizarre people and did so many things that I would never do at home. Somehow, having a passport not only gives you the freedom to go into other countries, but it also gives you the sense of freedom to be whoever you want to be. Hey, I was single, alone . . . and very blonde! "Mi perdoni padre, perche' ho peccato." *Forgive me, father, for I have sinned.*

I kept a journal of my travels so that by the time I landed back at LAX, I would have a whole novel's worth of my experiences overseas. This would prove to be very handy later on, when I realized that I indeed had a one-woman show in this journey.

Several years later, I collaborated on my one-woman play, *In Search of Fellini*, with writer Peter Kjenaas and celebrated having accomplished my personal mission. Playing some fourteen characters, I became "The Front Desk Guy" in Milan who wanted to be my permanent "companion." I became Pierre, the sweet, clean street-cleaner, who fell in love with me in front of Juliet's balcony in Verona. I became Michaelangelo, the faux artist with a phony line. Then there was Bippi, the antiques dealer who took me for a ride; and Cosmo, a toothless bum who spoke seven languages and had a dream of uniting the world. And finally, Mario, Fellini's "sidekick," who pretty much kept me from meeting this "man of my dreams."

I never did meet Fellini. But what difference did it make? I was *living* a Fellini film! But the funny thing is that I still had the same considerations when I got back from Italy that I had before I left. I still felt an indescribable gnawing inside of me, a feeling of wanting to say something important but not knowing how to go about doing it. I felt like there was a message to be delivered, but I wasn't sure what that message was. All I knew was that I was just going to continue in the same direction I was headed—it seemed to be the smart thing to do and I'd been successful at it so far.

This brings us back to why I wrote this book. A lot of the pilgrimages I had along the way were very Bart-like in their manifestation because they were risky, a bit mischievous, but always done in fun. And a lot of them just had to do with the simple fact that I am a girl from Ohio who had a dream. I consider myself one lucky gal, either way. It has been a long journey—a quest, if you will, seeking adventures and opportunities that inspire my "inner voice," even if that voice comes in the shape of a ten-year-old boy!

Just Another Job...

I got Bart on Tuesday, March 13, 1987. I didn't have the slightest pre-monition that the audition I had penned into my date book would lead to anything.

The day had a basic start up: glance at self in mirror, avoid scale, go to the Sports Connection for aerobics. I zipped over in my fully loaded navy blue with cream interior '84 Prelude and did tummy crunches to "Billy Jean" with the other girls, both female and male. The "Sports Erection" was in "Boys' Town," West Hollywood, and cross-gender hatred of cellulite was tolerated, actually encouraged. This was before step and Tae-Bo workouts, before infomercials and Slim•Fast. These were the innocent days of Jane Fonda and "Thriller," the days of sweat. Spandex was a definite style choice, mostly black, and worn as tight as a condom.

Two of my co-religionists in the struggle with fat were the five-foot-nine Wrigley twins. They had real names, but with their elegant legs and perfect busts, their glowing hair follicles and sweatless lashes, I always thought of them as the Wrigley twins. Double your pleasure. I would station myself between them, bookends for my five-foot-one frame, which carried about fifteen more pounds than they did—not combined, thank-you-very-much. Madonna, who had long since stopped acting "like a virgin," was also in the class. She kept to herself while we whooped and panted. After a shower and more reflection avoidance, I went for the audition that would change my life forever.

Getting the audition itself was a direct result of a general I had had with Bonita "Bonnie" Pietila, a casting director, several months earlier. A "general" means that you sit down in a low-pressure meeting and try to convince a person who can ultimately get you work that you can act without acting. It's an exercise in using conversation as a substitute for performance. I don't know what most people get out of them but some casting people still take them and all actors want them. I was no different. What I wanted was that amorphous "relationship" that could give me a break. I wanted my on-camera work to explode and eclipse my voice-over career. I saw Bonnie as a potential avenue, a freeway perhaps, to fulfill my ambitions of becoming the next Holly Hunter. My vision of the meeting had us talking intelligently about films, roles, casting choices, where I fit in. We would sip coffee and throw our heads back in easy laughter at some interesting anecdote about the industry. I was never nervous at these things so I knew she would be impressed. It was a fine day to take a giant leap toward the silver screen.

It was 1:45 and I had to hurry over the hill to meet her. (Going "over the hill" means that you're going either from the West Side of Los Angeles to the Valley, Burbank, Studio City, etc., or vice versa. Both of these areas are so vast that a wagon train would take two weeks to make the journey. Depending on traffic, it still does take about that long.) I arrived, did a quick brush-up and lipstick, as I am naturally natural, and went in to chit-chat.

All I knew about Bonnie was that she had once been an agent and my agent had set up the general. She was very cordial. Bonnie struck me as what I now think of as a Gap girl. She had an air of success and interest about her that was very professional. At that time I was balancing some on-camera work with tons of behind-the-mike work. I was also a dedicated student at the Beverly Hills Playhouse in Milton Katselas's acting class. This was a golden opportunity to impress Bonnie. I had been working on a scene from Tennessee Williams's *A Streetcar Named Desire.* I was Stella, opposite Dorothy Lyman's (*Mama's Family*) Blanche. We had been working on it for weeks. I was an artiste! . . . and certainly that would be obvious. Naturally, Stella was brushed aside and the conversation shifted over and tracked on my most unlikely of career niches. Bonnie had never met anyone typecast as a Little Pony, a Snork or a Glo-Friend. "Hello, Bonnie, and welcome to my world!"

The "ten-minute meeting" stretched out. It crossed my mind that I might not be impressing her with my ability to be in the next *Broadcast News* as I entertained her with dripping water sound effects and elephant sneezes. Whenever I tried to steer the conversation back to my Oscar-potential roles ("I've got a great scene partner . . .") we would end up back in the world of neighing steeds and fart noises. Voice-over work is highly sought after by on-camera actors because it pays so well for so little time. My career intrigued her immensely. We clicked for that moment in time. I was sure that we would meet again—and probably not in the land of Tennessee Williams.

Back to the future: Bart. I got the fateful call from my agent about an audition on the Fox lot for a funky little deal on *The Tracey Ullman Show*. And yes, Bonnie Pietila was the casting director. She remembered. This is so gratifying to an actor that it's difficult to describe. It's akin to the feeling you get when an uncle you saw once in the summer of '63 dies and leaves you money. Later, as we basked in our mutual good fortune as groundbreakers in the world of prime-time animation, she told me that mine was such a unique story that I was one of the first actors she had called. Okay, it's not *Broadcast News*, but Holly Hunter, eat your heart out!

They were looking for the voices for some animated "interstitials," or rather "bumpers," that were sandwiched between the commercial breaks and the show itself. These would be about thirty seconds to a minute long and they sometimes preceded the ads and sometimes followed. (I know you've always wanted to know what an "interstitial" is and now you do!) I was already working on about eight syndicated shows at the time, so to me it was just another audition.

I popped in my inspirational tape, Rick James's "She's a Super Freak." *"She's a very kinky girl, the kind you won't take home to mothaaaa . . ."* and cruised over the hill. I remember arriving about fifteen minutes early and sitting in the stark, hand-me-down furniture waiting area. (Actors become accustomed to waiting-room decor that is either the ratty remnants of some bygone set or office furniture rescued from some scrap heap. No offense.) There on the table were the monologues for each character. Because I was reading for the part of Lisa Simpson, I quickly shuffled through the stack and found the material for her: a monologue, neatly centered on the page, about five inches long, with accompanying character description.

Lisa's description was rather mundane:

Age: 8
Role in family: Middle child

That was about it. "Hmm," I thought. "Not much teeth." Little did I know that she would be a musical prodigy mentored by Bleeding Gums Murphy. She would have the integrity of Gandhi by refusing to eat meat, even though everyone else "had a cow, man." She would stand up for what she believed in and would even drop a dime on those who didn't abide by the law. She even went so far as to turn in her own father for illegally hooking up their television to cable. With the brilliant wit of the writers and the wry, in-your-eye, honest-to-a-fault interpretation, Yeardley Smith has made Lisa Simpson a bright light of leadership, full of compassion and competence beyond her years. Lisa Simpson is the kind of child we not only want our children to be, but also the kind of child we want *all* children to be. But at the time, on *The Tracey Ullman Show*, she was just an animated eight-year-old kid who had no personality.

Cut to Bart's five inches of fame.

"Aaaaaha! Now this is more like it!"

Age: 10

Personality: Devious, underachieving, school-hating, irreverent, clever

This was right up my alley and next to the Dumpster behind the greasy spoon. Not that I'm underachieving, school-hating or irreverent, mind you, but they are *so* much fun to play. And "clever" and "devious" rise up in the heart of any actor who sees a description like that. I tossed the Lisa part aside and began to study Bart's monologue. The content of that original monologue is lost to me. I can't recall at all what Bart's first words were, but most likely it had something to do with terrorizing Lisa and being choked by Homer.

Beside the monologue on the table, for artistic stimulation, were early character sketches. Early on, Bart had a sharper, more angular quality. He was clearly devious and about as sweet as a truck tire. He came to me immediately. I never had a doubt or another choice. I never considered that the voice I had chosen for him might be wrong. Typically, when auditioning for a part, I will give the producer or casting director a number of choices; our ideas may not match on the first try. But not with Bart. I knew him. There was no second guessing about it.

Bonnie ushered me into the tiny office, decorated in post-clearance sale to offset the military green walls. She sat off to one side and I took a seat across the metal table from Matt Groening, the creator. We shook hands.

Perhaps, in retrospect, I should capitalize the Creator, now that we know what an extraordinary feat Matt has accomplished. I have no idea, but I wonder if he knew, sitting there listening to actors voice his creations, that he was on the verge of such unprecedented success. Or was it "just another creation" for him? Matt sat there, comfortable and casual, in beard and glasses. I knew nothing about him or about his comic strip, *Life Is Hell*, which had captured the eye of director-producer James L. Brooks. I knew nothing about the now legendary meeting in which Matt had scribbled out the Simpsons characters off the top of his head in just fifteen minutes and started this most unlikely of journeys.

It was time to play. There wasn't a lot of chit-chat. We cut right to the chase.

"I know I'm supposed to read for Lisa, but I'd much rather read for Bart. Do you mind?"

He didn't. He hadn't made any hard decisions on the casting and was completely open-minded to whatever the talent brought in. So I gave it a shot.

Matt cracked up. "That's it! That's Bart!"

And I was offered the part on the spot! I'd like to say that I was chosen out of thousands—it impresses the folks and especially your agent if you're auditioning with 3,000 other actors! But, turns out, I was the only one to read for Bart . . . Cowabunga!

"Hey, We're Recording Up Here!"

Starting in the spring of '87, Julie Kavner, Dan Castellaneta, Yeardley Smith and I gathered about once a week to record the Simpsons "shorts" or "bumpers," if you will, for *The Tracey Ullman Show*. We wedged ourselves into a tiny room, looked each other over, double-checked our armpits and got down to it.

The hierarchy of producers and creative staff we have come to rely on over the years may have existed in those days but you would never have known it. Matt, our Creator, must have been thrilled to have the opportunity to air something on prime time, but the whole thing was something of a lark, hardly on a par with a "real" series. There was that audition and then he, like the rest of us, probably didn't have a clue that these tiny vignettes would ever develop into a planetary-wide craze, capturing audiences from age two on up; entertaining them not only with the weekly series and all the syndicated episodes you can program your VCR to tape, but also with a billion-dollar merchandise-generating extravaganza, ranging from backpacks and talking dolls to key chains and Bart Bread! Believe me, everyone was surprised.

Fox had worked hard to create its reputation, a reputation for doing things differently; a reputation designed to snare a "lost audience" that had no home. It was the only card they had to play, after all, fighting the uphill battle against "The Eye," "The Peacock," and "The Alphabet Web"—the reigning networks. They laughed and kicked sand in Fox's face, as Fox had not yet established itself as a viable competitor in the marathon for ratings. The Simpsons bumpers were just an attempt to pull in an audience, to try something unique that had never been done before in an industry where "everything had been done before." There was no crystal ball, no media guru who prognosticated what this would become. Vegas gave no odds.

Compared to the recording digs Springfield has today, our beginnings were less than humble. Now that we are truly "prime time," we have all that money and techno-geeks can provide. But the video engineer's booth at soundstage 17 where we laid down the early bumpers was more on a par with some kind of frat challenge—twenty guys and a Volkswagen. The only thing that the high-tech world of today and our spartan booth of the distant past share is the smell of the mike—that never changes.

Typically, a voice-over gig is done at a recording studio, which is broken up into individual recording spaces, designed for *recording* voice-overs for radio, television, film, etc. Each space has two units: a soundproof booth for the performer/s and a control booth filled with outrageous gadgets called mixers. These mixers presumably mix and I presume they mix sound. The director typically sits in there, on the other side of the glass from us performers, and says things that we hear through our headsets like, "Can you do that again? Just one more time." And, of course, he'll say that several times. The producer, also in attendance, nods along sagely with this wise direction and then they both await the skilled hands of the engineer, who sets everything up. There can be more engineers, more producers and such, but that's the basic mix.

These engineers, by the way, have a sweat-free job. There are no ladders, sets nor lights to move so you never get the old "gaffer's crack" when the guy with encrusted jeans lifts several tons of cable. No, your sound engineer will gently reach out over your shoulder and reset your microphone. "Do you prefer to stand or sit?" he'll ask. With him will come the scent of Irish Spring. I love these guys—Brad Brock, Ron Cox, Terry Brown—efficient, friendly, casually dressed guys on a tight schedule. Theirs is an air-conditioned world.

Now that you have that lovely image of what a sound booth is *supposed* to be like, you can pretty much forget about it and imagine six people crammed in an elevator. Not to give anyone the impression that "we walked to work every day, ten miles through driving snow . . ." but soundstage 17 *was not designed* for voice-over production. It was designed for rehearsing and taping/filming television and film productions.

Taking up most of the space was the actual set for *The Tra-*

cey Ullman Show. This brilliantly crafted, modern-day *Carol Bur-nett Show* was a sketch comedy and the set changed from week to week. Facing the set there was an arc-shaped area for the cameras to operate in and, behind the cameras, bleachers for the audience. Way, way up on top of the bleachers, in the nosebleed section where no one catches a home run, was the booth for the "techies" and producer/executive. It was not that big; revise that, it was small . . . something a sardine would love. During the taping of the show the sound engineer spends his time tuning monitors that look like they belong in some train station. He makes sure everything is recording properly by touching buttons and knobs. It's magic. Network executives, those guys in designer suits, don't really hang out in this booth during the taping because effective pacing requires more space, and nail-biting and excessive grinning can cause the monitors to malfunction. This miniature booth was considered a perfect fit for producing the Simpsons bumpers, and it was, as long as the fire marshal never dropped by and I kept up with the Wrigley twins.

The early recordings were done in a typically makeshift Simpsons fashion—a scheme that Homer might think up if there were easy money in it and if it involved doughnuts. When they weren't rehearsing or taping the "real" actors downstairs, and there was no audience to contend with, *and* things were supposed to be relatively quiet, they would schedule us to come in. The engineer would tack up some of those heavy mover's carpets to the booth walls and hang more to cover the window overlooking the sound-stage. (Now that I think of it, this was a bit of a sweat job and maybe there was a gaffer's crack moment or two.) I think this grad student method was used in an effort to economize, but it could also have been a reluctance on the part of the producers to acknowledge the fact that we existed at all. "What animation?! Oh, that little thing?" What we were doing was unprecedented when we hit the airwaves. It might bomb and then "that thing they did up in the booth" could be easily forgotten.

We four actors would squeeze into our corner of the tiny booth. Then Paul Germaine, the voice-director, would wedge in. And, finally, the engineer, who recorded us on a portable tape deck he probably got for Christmas, slid in to complete the package. Oh, but wait! I'm forgetting something. *What about the scripts?* I hear the sound of a 500-pound soundproof studio door slamming and the dull *thud-thud-thud* of footsteps rapidly approaching. (Drumroll, please.) It's Super-Matt, to the rescue! Hurtling toward us like a shot out of a cannon, Matt would bound up the steps into the ozone where we all awaited the arrival of the new vignettes with bated breath. Now we were all ready to go. We were barricaded in there for a couple hours at a time, sharing two microphones and jockeying for position whenever our characters spoke. Sometimes the noise from "downstairs," as grips and gaffers cranked up their rock and roll to do a setup, would rumble in the booth. "Hey. We're recording up here!" We would get mystified looks in response as if some lesser god had spoken from some lesser heaven. Then someone with a carpenter's belt would amble over and kill Van Halen. I thought it was all pretty silly. Loved it, actually. This was our humble beginning and we had a ball.

These were great days for me, drinking up first impressions of my fellow cast members and savoring their talent. I believe that

I was the only one who had done voice-overs at the time, at least extensively. But the other actors took to it like ducks to other ducks. Julie Kavner was the only cast member I knew much about and only from the standpoint of a fan. I had loved her on *Rhoda* and a bit later when she played an executive assistant to Woody Allen in his film *Hannah and Her Sisters*. And, of course, most recently, she was the Ethel Mertz to Tracey Ullman's Lucy Ricardo. She was and continues to be a workhorse of an actor, one to admire and emulate. Okay, I admit it . . . I was a bit starstruck. "Wow! What is she doing *this* for?!" I watched her work and was immediately impressed by her extraordinary professionalism and quiet work ethic. (I believe, in the entire twelve-year history of the Simpsons, from bumpers through the TV show, to date, Julie has been late once, and she damned near died of shame when she finally showed up. I don't recall why she was late, but I have an image of a wet cat—either Julie herself, drenched in a Southern California downpour, or her actual cat, if she has a cat.) She stepped up to the mike and delivered that odd, rare, fantastic voice that somehow evokes the quintessential mom with just the right dash of wry cartoon humor. I grinned from ear to ear when she first spoke and do so to this day.

Yeardley was very shy at first in the social setting but not when facing that mike. I was awed by the simple adjustment she made to her natural voice to become the eight-year-old Lisa. Adjusting, in some form, is what acting is all about and making a small change is no small feat. The subtle art of adjusting one's natural vocal delivery is something that many actors strive to accomplish but few truly master. Yeardley has always made it look, and sound, so effortless and as she created those initial moments, which were, for the most part, lines dealing with Bart's reign of terror, you could sense the lurking genius that she would bring out in the character.

Dan was the biggest surprise of all in terms of contrast. He amazed me the first day when this incredibly nice guy, a real Clark Kent, turned to the microphone and burped up Homer. That was just the first of many Super Voice-over Dan transformations we have witnessed.

In between our recordings, I had time to watch Tracey's show being taped. I was a fast fan. Tracey's a Brit, but you might never know it, because the broad characterizations she is so talented in creating and delivering completely disguise the fact. I'd stretch out on my living room floor in my little Burbank place, alone in the human company department, with my newest family members, McGuffy, the giant-eared, pint-sized perennial puppy, and Lydia, the loving Golden. We would munch popcorn—I thought popcorn was fiber—and giggle through the show. Tracey was a pop-star-turned-actress and I loved best of all her thirteen-year-old-girl with the braces, Jessica. She metamorphosed into this teen with gay parents, played by Dan Castellaneta and Sam Mc-Murray. Such a cool kid—bright, witty, with these great comebacks. I admired both Tracey and her character. I wanted to establish myself the same way. I just needed a big break! I can do what she does!

The recordings were great fun, even if I felt a bit like the tolerated stepchild of Tracey's show, not disliked so much as never brought into the inner circle, the world beyond the glass, never invited to the Prince's ball. Because Julie and Dan were regulars in the live show, I'm sure this feeling was one that I shared with myself. At times I'd show up early, to be "noticed," though I would never have admitted it. I was there in the unlikely event that a guest star wouldn't show, perhaps be kidnapped or in a car wreck or suffer a diva tantrum. They would need someone right then. "Who can we get to play this part?!" the director would scream. "I need an actress!" It would be just like a Fred Astaire movie, a spotlight on Nancy as she descends to the rescue. "Excuse me, sir . . ." I'd show him my time step, and that would be that.

In the *real* world I would perch in the bleachers and watch "them," the legitimate actors, blocking a scene, laughing conspiratorially over some moment. I'd watch, thinking, I should get a part on this series! I'm right here! It never became an obsession, really no more than the rampant desires of my overactive imagination, painting pictures of that elusive opportunity, that "break."

Who am I kidding? I wanted to be on the show so badly I could tap dance in my sleep. One week, while pretending to read something in the bleachers, I came up with a bright idea. (I do this now and then.) In an opportune quiet moment I approached one of the Tracey Ullman producers. Uh oh . . . a guy in a suit. Red flag! The suit was a dead giveaway. (Equation for all young actors: Slick suit plus winning smile does not equal a mother's love.) I asked him if I could do Bart in the live audience warm-up act. It was all part of my grand scheme to achieve stardom. After a raised eyebrow and a shrug he gave me the go ahead.

This had to be one of the most mortifying experiences of my life and even more so because it took me completely by surprise.

Lacking an open bar, most half-hours that are taped before a live audience have some kind of warm-up act. In this case, as in most, it was a stand-up comedian. His face is completely blocked out in my memory, like some shirtless suspect with his features bleeped out on the latest episode of *Cops*. He sized me up like a hungry shark and agreed to work me into his gig. Big mistake. I expected the audience, that sea of faces filling the bleachers, to be somehow fascinated with my role behind the scenes. Apparently there was a "buzz" already about our quirky animated family. He introduced me and I stepped out, all bright and sunny . . . and became a natural disaster in about two seconds. "Who is this woman, anyway?" was written all over their collective faces and my knees went dry and my tongue got wobbly. It must have been obvious to the stand-up, whoever he was, that I was dying inside, because he started having fun with whatever it was I said, zinging off it and chipping away at what little confidence was keeping me upright. The entire experience from ". . . the voice of Bart Simpson, Nancy Cartwright . . ." forward, what was no more than about two minutes in the real universe but which stretched out to Einsteinian-proportions for me, is blocked out, covered under layers of terror. I have no problem acting, but stepping out there with nothing on but my own desire to impress was far worse than being stark naked! Not only was I not funny, I don't even think I got any courtesy laughs. So much for stardom!

Jack Lemmon once said that an artist must not only "get naked" in front of an audience but he must also "turn around veeeeeery slowly." Let's face it, the public wasn't quite ready for "naked Bart." I made as quick an exit as I could with clenched gluteus maximus and as I was passing that producer he scoffed, "Your baby sister's name is Maggie, not Lisa." God only knows what I said up there!

All in all, this debacle to the contrary, it was great fun. As the weeks ticked by, the stepchild energy ironically reversed. The Nielsen word on the street was that we, the Simpsons, were picking up a following, even as Tracey's show waned a bit in popularity. A curious phenomenon. I'm sure Tracey felt this unique shift in attention and didn't like it. (Historical vindication: To date, HBO's *Tracey Takes On* series has received no less than nine nominations and eleven awards, including the Golden Globe, the Glaad Media Award, SAG Award, DGA Award, the Emmy, the American Comedy Award, the Cable Ace Award and the Golden Satellite. You go, girl!)

As we picked up steam, an ever-increasing number of America's finest tuned in and munched fiber along with me. They tuned in and waited to see the commercials—a sponsor's wet dream—in order to catch this wacky animated family that existed around car ads and programming blurbs. Many viewers were channel surfing from the latest *Murder, She Wrote,* a good wholesome show, to catch our bumpers. They'd eye this messed-up family where the dad gulped beer, belched and choked his son with abandon. "Isn't that awful!" they would cry out in social indignation, while they clandestinely preset their remotes in preparation for the next commercial. Then it was back to Angela Lansbury as she solved another murder that happened at yet another cousin's wedding.

In my little world, McGuffy would sit beside me and sometimes cock an ear at the set when Bart started gagging in Homer's grasp. It's not that I sound like Bart in real life—we'll get to that never-ending battle later—but maybe to a dog, a voice is like a scent: You can't cover it up. My family back in Ohio couldn't get the show yet—no Fox affiliate, so I didn't have to deal with any potential negative reactions from that corner. A couple of my closest friends expressed guarded opinions about it being "too violent," but when pressed, they had to admit that it didn't keep them from surfing over. I was part of a cult hit!

After completing about thirty-five shorts, rumor had it that Fox was going to take a chance on us and extend the idea into a full half-hour . . . or twenty-three minutes if you deduct the commercial breaks. The growing public of "outsiders" was eating us up and washing us down with Duff beer. The audience seemed to be there, but taking a chance of this magnitude on such a strange beast is no small gamble in network television. For any show to get picked up as a regular series takes a huge financial commitment. In this case it was going to take millions of dollars to create the entire "assembly line" to deliver the product, pulling together a huge multinational animation team. And, of course, this would mean adding a few new "members" to the Simpson family—Hank Azaria, Pamela Hayden, Tress MacNeille, Maggie Roswell, Harry Shearer, Russi Taylor and Marcia Wallace. It was a leap of faith that required some courage, I'm sure. Heads roll in the networks when the belly flops. This show had to be outstanding!

The rumor became a contract and all doubts as to whether we would do it were vanquished. We were going where few had dared to go before: prime-time animation! It was an electrifying prospect and everyone climbed on the Springfield bandwagon. Personally, I had no doubts from the very beginning that this was going to go somewhere, but no one, including myself, foresaw the entertainment goldmine it would become. This animated anomaly would be popular, yes, but *never* a household word. *Never* would we be honored with a Peabody Award, fifteen Emmy Awards, twelve Annie Awards, three Genesis Awards, seven International Monitor Awards and four Environmental Media Awards, among numerous other nods. *Never* would Bart Simpson, along with Charlie Chaplin, Steven Spielberg, Oprah Winfrey, Lucille Ball, Frank Sinatra, Louis Armstrong and T. S. Eliot, be recognized as "One of the Top Artists and Entertainers of the Twentieth Century," according to *Time* magazine. And *never* would the Simpsons receive a star on the Hollywood Walk of Fame! Come on, people, this is a cartoon!!!

We said good-bye to Tracey in 1989. During the downtime, before we came back to record our first half-hour episode, Fox set up our *big*, real McCoy, recording studio. It would be complete with soundproof glass separator, mixers galore sporting oodles of dials and diodes, and more electrified engineers than you can shake a script at.

While this creative orgy was in full swing, I had far more important things to attend to on my personal plate. I had a wedding to plan following my recent elopement so we could get some juicy gifts. And I had a baby to make with my new husband, Warren Murphy.

Good Grammer

I have saved a lifetime of date books, journals and even packed away written reports from the fourth grade. Now that I have a couple of kids of my own, these reports have come in handy for last-minute homework assignments! No, no, no . . . don't get me wrong. My kids still do their own homework. I just find it extremely helpful to show them that they aren't the only ones who had to figure out Ghana's annual rainfall and the native birds of the Yucatan Peninsula. I have saved papers from the second grade, when I was learning how to write in cursive. I have a drawing of the complete circulatory system, which I was tested on in Mr. MacKelvey's seventh-grade class. My date books are particularly special because I can go back to any ol' time I want. Plus, I figure these diaries might come in handy if I ever get hit with a subpoena or a warrant for imitating a ten-year-old.

Here's one: *Friday morning, 11:00, Dec. 19, 1976 ... performed as the Monotone Angel in the annual Christmas show at Fairmont West. Note: During the performance, while suspended above the entire choir, the cable breaks and I literally go flying. Asked later what they remember most about me, the response is unanimous, "Falling and choking the entire soprano section and turning a charming holiday tradition into a vaudeville farce."* Yes, I remember it well.

I came across a diary entry that I wrote way back in the late eighties at the very beginnings of *The Simpsons*. Check out what was going on inside my mind ... and no, I was not into glamrock.

▶ SEPTEMBER 18, 1989

THIS *is our eleventh show of the* first *season. I say "first" because I really think this show is* amazing! *There is absolutely* nothing *like* The Simpsons, *now or ever. Nope, this is not your run-of-the-mill family. This quirky unit: father, mother, sisters and brother may be animated but they somehow represent every family that I have ever known, especially mine! Okay, my dad didn't choke my brother over dinner and my mother's blue hair didn't scrape the ceiling, but we had a loyalty to one another no matter how much strangling, smirking and belching went on.* All in the Family *may have been as irreverent and blatantly in-your-face, but nothing has ever come close in the world of animation. Who knows what will happen in the seasons to come. I can just see Bart suddenly elected president of the Student Council . . . God help the little children, or Lisa being chosen as an Ambassador of Goodwill for the United Nations . . . world peace at last! I guess we'll just have to see. All I know for now is that I am loving this and I am loving being Bart!*

I am so inspired I've decided to begin my personal memoirs regarding this show. There simply has to be a record of what's going on! Who knows? Maybe some day I'll actually get around to writing a book! It was having Kelsey Grammer as a guest on the show today that got me going. I'll bet he's the first of many. I know the "guest" game. I have been a "guest star" on numerous television shows, including Mr. Belvedere, Empty Nest, *and even worked with Kelsey on* Cheers. *(I accused him of being a kleptomaniac, which he didn't take very kindly . . . Dr. Crane, that is.) I had a super time being on his show, but I was definitely "The Guest." I felt like I was in first gear, rip-roarin' ready to act, but the regular cast was cruisin' along in overdrive, already comfortable with their characters and what they were doing. (I wonder if he senses any kind of a "gear change"—moving from being a star on* Cheers *to being a guest star on* The Simpsons. *) Regardless, it's cool to have the shoe on the other foot. Who's next? I wonder? The buzz is that there are a lot of celebrities working their agents to get into Springfield. That is so way cool.*

It makes me wonder how the writers will use these animation-hungry celebs? Will parts be created for them, like with Kelsey, or will they be lampooning themselves, so to speak? How about a story where Lisa hooks up with the new girl in school and have Goldie Hawn do the voice? Or some old fart comes to town to teach disco at the local college? John Travolta in Spring-field Night Fever. *"Stayin' Alive" would take on a whole new meaning. I heard he has a good sense of humor and he'd probably love that.*

WELL, we never did get John or Goldie but the stars kept falling into the sound booth. Kelsey was the first guest star to actually work with us on the show. Penny Marshall is credited as number one. She loaned us her voice as the lunatic baby-sitter, Mrs. Botz, but her schedule didn't coordinate so, alas, it was done in a private session. Way, way back in 1993 Fox put together a "Behind-the-Scenes-of-the-Simpsons" for a sales presentation. Jim Brooks said, "We have people that you can't get on the phone who call us to be on the show. It's been great." And it's still great. The calls just keep on comin'! As the millennium turns, we've had a record-breaking 238 guest stars! I wish that I could tell you that I have worked with each and every one of them and became their closest, most personal best friend . . . "Oh, Hef, long time no see. How is the remodeling on the breasts, er, mansion coming along? Oh, hold on a minute, call-waiting . . . Hello? Oh, hi Bette! So what do you think? You, me, Michelle, Susan and Kim? Yes? Oh, great! I'll make sure they leave David, Tim and Alec at home . . . No, little Ronnie Howard cannot come!" But alas, t'would be a lie! I have worked with a handful of celebrities, as has each member of the cast. It depends, for the most part, on the script and who has lines with whom. The rest depends entirely on the star's avail-ability—and, how do I say this?—attitude?

What can I say? Celeb sessions are . . . unique. First off, most of the recordings happen around the actor's schedule. It's a cell phone world. The celebs just work the recording of their lines around their schedule. We rarely meet. It is as much a surprise to me as to the regular fan. Often times we won't even know which celeb they got until the show airs. "Omygod! Honey, look who's on the show!" Bart is talking to Sting! And we never met. Bummer. Hey, it's Johnny Carson! Or Bette Midler or the Red Hot Chili Peppers! But of the celebs we got to "play with," most were absolutely wonderful. Some were delightful. A few were not particularly memorable. And one was . . . (oops, this is not that kind of book!) Suffice it to say, working with celebrities added a whole new dimension to the show.

On the surface you'd think that being a guest on *The Simpsons* would be a walk in Springfield Park. Just show up . . . no lines to memorize, no makeup, no hair, no wardrobe considerations. You just get a mike check, give the director a few takes and go off to meet Spielberg at Spago! No rehearsal, maybe not even a table read. No lights, "hitting your marks" or Craft Services snack choices to make. Butterfinger (*shameless self-promotion!*) or Power Bar? It doesn't matter because we don't *have* Craft Services. (We get a table chock-full of the same doughnuts, bagels and fruit—replaced weekly, of course—I hope.) But for those who come into our world, the pressure in our little studio can get to the Megastar. Sometimes they sweat. Sometimes they put their foot in their mouth. And sometimes they don't say a whole lot except what is written right in front of them. The "why" of it always fascinates me.

Here we are, a bunch of actors doing a cartoon. Easy. This gig has become a thread in the overall fabric of our careers. It's a "job," albeit a fantastic one, and we know one another so well. We know Springfield, the style. There are still surprises, like when Dan adds an improv lick to Homer's latest escapade. But we are so at home that we take "trouble" in stride. "Hank's not here today? Working on his fifth movie in a row?" No problem. "Julie's in another off-Broadway show?" Cool. "Yeardley's on so-and-so this week?" She rules. "Harry's doing what?!" And then there's me, "Nancy's got laryngitis?" Bummer. It's very casual. "Potty break!" (Okay, I am the only actor who does that. But then again, I have kids so I have an excuse.) You get the idea.

But it's totally reversed for a guest. When they show up, they're on *our* turf. "Sure you won the Oscar for *Braveheart,* but what can you do *here?*" It's like the first day of school in a new town. These celebs are expected to perform—and I don't just mean the character they are playing. It's "Show me" time in Springfield and many of them feel that pressure.

Some just do the gig without a hitch. Danny DeVito, for instance, just fit right in to Springfield. You could imagine his character, Herb Powell, open a new car lot on Main Street right between Moe's Tavern and Apu's Kwik-E-Mart. On some occasions we get a total rookie, someone who has never done voice-overs before. "Hey, Mack! That's the mike right there!" That has got to be tough. Just the idea that you are dealing with a "family" that has been together for upward of ten years and that everyone is watching you to see if you're good or you suck is pretty staggering; then add to that an unfamiliarity with the territory itself and I can only imagine the pressure. "Is this mike on?!" Tap, tap, tap. Sheesh.

▼   ▼   ▼

I remember Luke Perry joining us when we were still recording in the basement of the Darryl Zanuck Theater. The soundstage there is huge. Luke was very casual but you could tell that he was thrilled to be a part of our cast, even if just temporarily. He shook a few hands—"Great show, you guys." That *90210* popular smile of his lit up the room. Hmm, not a bad-lookin' kisser. Perry guest starred as himself playing the never-introduced-before brother of Sideshow Mel. His character wears an old-fashioned leather helmet and a white suit with his name in sequins across his chest. Sideshow Luke is shot out of a cannon and goes flying through a window in the back of the auditorium, screaming all the way. The action in the recorded script has him hit the pavement and slide, nearly getting run over by a car. But Perry's performance was so awesome the writers and animators were able to go absolutely ballistic, taking his scream into uncharted territories, literally. You'd never know it though, unless you had a copy of the script right in front of you. (And my scripts are not available, so don't *even* send those letters.) When you check out the episode ultimately seen by America, "Krusty Gets Kancelled," you'll see poor Luke go from the car slamming on its brakes, then flying through yet another window . . . of a sandpaper factory! (Again with the screaming!) Then, out the other side, through the doors of the Kwik-E-Mart, finally crashing into a pyramid display of cans that Apu had just completed stacking. *Thud!* He's down on the ground, moaning, "My face! My valuable face!"

There's always a certain amount of voyeuristic curiosity in having a star on the show, another source of pressure for the guest. I can go to the mall and only rarely (like never) will someone run up and ask for Bart's autograph—you have to be a pretty serious fan to recognize me in my unanimated form. But you'd have to live in a cave somewhere not to recognize Michael Jackson. It has been a fascinating study in human behavior to notice how this observation not only affects the star him- or herself, but also how it affects each of us. I'm the big fan, Yeardley is polite, Dan is reserved, Julie is a total pro, Hank is just a regular guy and as for Harry, well . . . he's just Harry.

IT'S not just the actors who can be starstruck. The Simpson scribes don't just throw a dart at Jim Brooks's wanna-be guest list. And it's their tastes, sick as they may be (!) that fans ultimately see and hear. Let's face it, they have a ball. In one of my favorite memories the "ball" they had was baseball. Part of the writing team of 1991 had a thing for the Dodgers. They championed fellow writer John Swartzwelder's "Homer at the Bat" with the Dodgers players in mind, hoping they would meet their idols, and players from other teams, in the process. And it worked! On the big day, the writers huddled together, practically drooling, shifting from foot to foot, anxious to shake some hands. Totally uncharacteristic. Absolutely charming. They were like eight-year-olds! Their normal "mellow" attitudes were nowhere to be seen, and there was even color in those computer-pale cheeks. There's nothing like the sight of a bunch of pro writers becoming kids again. In walked Darryl Strawberry, Steve Sax, Wade Boggs, Jose Canseco, Roger Clemens, Ken Griffey, Jr., Don Mattingly, Mike Scioscia and Ozzie Smith. The writers suddenly made me feel like I was back in the fourth grade surrounded by a pack of Bart Simpsons!

With a successful "baseball career" in place, the next season's writers went one better. They were *huge* Adam West fans. "Hey, let's bring in the Caped Crusader! Yeah!" It was a real hoot and quite a surprise to see a dozen writers line up to get Batman's autograph! (Months later, after the show, "Mr. Plow," aired, the only complaint that Adam West had was "They didn't make me look more like Tom Cruise!")

The writers create parts for two types of guests: those that play themselves and those that take on a character. Adam West was one of the multitude of talents who were willing to poke fun at themselves. You've got to hand it to them, this is one of the true tests of a really cool dude! Don't get me wrong, I think it is good to respect yourself, but to cooperate in a public satire of your own personal characteristics, beliefs or passions marks you as a good sport who doesn't take life soooooooo seriously.

Phone call from CAA (Creative Artists Agency—one of the "Top Ten" agencies that represent actors, directors and writers) to his star: "Hey, *The Simpsons* wants you to be on their show. No, they want you to play yourself. They want you to be willing to be publicly humiliated, pointing out some of your obvious personal flaws and sign an agreement that you won't sue. What do you think?" I'd just jump at the chance, wouldn't you!? The odd truth is, now that we are established as *the* show to be on, the answer is usually, "Yes!" Larry King will mock his show just to beat Charlie Rose to the punch! Do you suppose John Glenn was upset when Buzz Aldrin appeared as himself? Twice?! I can just imagine the phone conversation he might have had with his representative: "Hey, Larry, Buzz was on *The Simpsons* last night. What's the deal, man? What do I hire you for anyway?!"

GETTING someone to appear on the show had never been a problem, at least until the spring of '99. In the episode "When You Dish Upon a Star," our producers had tried and tried to convince a number of celebrity couples to be on the show. This was one of the most difficult shows to cast because it required both the husband and wife to be well-known stars. It got to be a real challenge, not only finding a Hollywood pair that were actually still married—sorry about that—but to find a pair who were both available to work! Tom and Nicole—still shooting *Eyes Wide Shut*; Bruce and Demi—not even a consideration; Ted and Jane—not a good idea. But when we heard that Alec Baldwin and Kim Basinger were not only happily married, but also available ... whooo-whoo! *Bingo!* We got ourselves a double-deal! They were absolutely hilarious. Their willingness to poke fun at themselves was so inspiring! In one of the scenes, Kim is holding her Oscar and turns to Homer and says, "Wow, you've got everything, Homer! Even the Oscar polish!" Then she opens a jar of polish and begins shining her statuette. Alec walks in on her and says, "Honey, why don't you give that thing a rest? You're taking the finish off." She, of course, has the last word, "When you win one, you can take care of it however you want." I'm sure! What a hoot! They were playful and giddy and absolutely in love with each other and being on the show.

I am sure that they were the envy of their friends, especially those who are celebrity couples. To actually be able to work together, as themselves, publicly airing their Evian-washed laundry ... what an honor! Some day their daughter will be old enough

Here are members of the elite club who have accepted the mantle of self-deprecation and appeared as themselves. In order of appearance: Tony Bennett, Larry King, Ringo Starr, Aerosmith, Sting, Steve Allen, Bob Hope, Adam West, Leonard Nimoy, Brooke Shields, Barry White, David Crosby, Johnny Carson, Hugh Hefner, Bette Midler, Luke Perry, The Red Hot Chili Peppers, George Harrison, The Ramones, Ernest Borgnine, Robert Goulet, Conan O'Brien, James Woods, James Taylor, Buzz Aldrin, Dr. Demento, Dennis Franz, Dick Cavett, Johnny Unitas, Mel Brooks, Tito Puente, Mickey Rooney, Paul and Linda McCartney, Paul Anka, Tom Kite, Bob Newhart, Suzanne Somers, Sonic Youth, Cypress Hill, Smashing Pumpkins, Peter Frampton, Michael Buffer, Tim Conway, Joe Namath, Roy Firestone, Stephen Jay Gould, Alex Trebek, Steven Wright, Janeane Garofalo, Bobcat Goldthwait, Bruce Baum, Jay Leno, Hank Williams Jr., Bob Denver, U2, Ed McMahon, Regis Philbin, Kathie Lee Gifford, Jerry Springer, Alec Baldwin, Kim Basinger, Ron Howard, Brian Grazer, and finally, Mel Gibson. Good sports, every one. (Whew. I need a cold beverage.)

to appreciate it, but certainly their friends and family got a kick out of seeing that episode.

It makes one wonder about the possible motivation behind deciding to do it. Alec already had a reputation for being a prankster and a fun guy to be around on a movie set. But what of those who don't necessarily have that reputation? Not that they are "trouble," mind you, but just that they are not known for being practical jokers. Some of the guests who have played themselves are better known for other qualities besides being silly, so our show offered them a chance to, perhaps, show the world that they too can make fun of themselves. When I think practical joker, I think Steve Martin, Woody Harrelson and Jim Varney, who all appeared as characters other than themselves.

When Michelle Pfeiffer

played Mindy Simmons, a nuclear plant co-worker, Homer had finally met his match. It wasn't that she ate as many doughnuts as he—and still kept her figure, dammit—and it wasn't that she took a power nap before lunch just as he. What really impressed me was that Mindy could actually belch out a Duff burp louder, deeper and more satisfyingly than Homer—and Michelle did her own sound effects! Now that, folks, is some seeeeeeerious comedy!

The list will certainly keep growing. We recently had Britney Spears over to play in Springfield—another guest who popped in and out when no one else was around. Boo hoo.

And then . . . there's Tom Jones. After he guest starred, he personally invited me and my husband and a couple of other couples to his show at the MGM Grand in Las Vegas. What a memorable night that was. After an incredible evening of being wined and dined and totally treated like a star, we were escorted backstage to the green room, where the artists hang out before and after a performance. We chit-chatted and nibbled from the assortment of yummy treats, toasted each other for the good times and soon Tom came in to join us. He was such a total stud! What a cool guy—before, during and after the show! I kept trying to tell him what a super show he had and how much we appreciated his hospitality and he just went on and on about *The Simpsons* and what a blast he had on our show and that his career totally went into an upswing *after* he had been a guest star! I believe his exact words were, "It pumped up my career!" How cool is that?!

The simple truth of the matter, I suppose, is that most of the celebs that we get to be on our show are just plain fans. Let's face it: It's hip to be on *The Simpsons*. Most of the stars that end up "taking a vacation" in Springfield have families. I don't have any doubt that they love being on the show because it is a hit, but more importantly I think they love the idea that they can do something that their kids think is cool. (And besides, they get to walk away with a bunch of door prizes!—a way-cool jacket, signed scripts and an assortment of merchandise usually not available anywhere!)

I get a little embarrassed when I look back at how I reacted to some of the guests. I didn't think that I was the awestruck-type. But you just can't predict those feelings sometimes. And I find it funny whom I reacted to and how. Some reactions were obvious: Mel's buns . . . oooooh. Others, like publicly embarrassing myself when Ernest Borgnine walked in the room by calling out, "Marty!" took me totally by surprise. I'd like to think that I have learned something, if only about my own attitudes. I've learned to chill . . . a bit. But I still feel like a representative of the masses, the great unknowns of the television audience. I'm there to get an autograph for the world, thank you very much.

I have gone through my own personal date books (I know, get a life, right?) to cull the most interesting celebrity experiences I have had on the show. They appear in chronological order so you can track right along with me as the popularity of the show increased. For now, let us take a journey back in Dr. Ludvig's time machine, back to our humble beginnings . . . at the start of this chapter.

*I*T *is September 18, 1989 . . . Kelsey faces the mike for the first time . . .*

Act One, Scene 1: We are inside a television studio, in Krusty's circus ring. We hear circus music. A spotlight hits a small

clown car that is driving into the ring. Krusty hops out. There is
a bleacher full of young children, who cheer wildly.

KRUSTY:

Hey, kids! Who do you love?

CHILDREN:

Krusty!

KRUSTY:

How much do you love me?

INT. SIMPSON LIVING ROOM—CONTINUOUS
Bart, Lisa and Maggie are sitting on the couch, watching Krusty on TV.

BART/LISA/CHILDREN:

With all our hearts!

KRUSTY:

What would you do if I went off the air?

BART/LISA/CHILDREN:

We'd kill ourselves!

I glance over at Kelsey and it's like a tennis match, all heads
swinging over to catch his reaction. He laughs, we crack up. This
is the power of a star. He is the one who sets the tone for the
room. And from that moment on, we had a blast. Every single

page had about three or four good laughs on it, and every single time, I found my eyes slipping over to check out Kelsey's reaction. As the story unfolded, Sideshow Bob is introduced, but we don't hear him speak until the middle of Act Two. Up until then, a simple slide-whistle has been his sole source of communication. Krusty is found "guilty" of stealing and Sideshow Bob is now in the center ring, taking over where Krusty left off. With his speech, he addresses the children:

SIDESHOW BOB:

My young friends. For years I have been silent save for the crude glissandos of this primitive wind instrument. But now destiny has thrust me into the center ring. In the coming weeks, you will notice some rather sweeping changes in our program. Please, do not be alarmed. Itchy and Scratchy will still have a home here, but we will also learn about nutrition, self-esteem, etiquette and all the lively arts.

By the end of this, we were all in stitches. Kelsey had put his own personal "voice-print" on this character and no one could take it away from him! He was bitter, sardonic and sarcastic and all to the delight of everyone in the room. There was no doubt about it, Kelsey had made his place in the family Simpson . . . er, I should say, Kelsey and his own personal one-man fan club, Sideshow Bob.

SIDESHOW Bob has since appeared six more times . . . I guess I wasn't the only one impressed!

T.S.O.P. (The Sound of Phil)

▶ JUNE 29, 1990

I got to the studio a little early today. No particular reason. It is always a crap shoot whether or not the freeway is jam-packed and backed up to another county or whether it is just bumper-to-bumper. I guess my timing was pretty good. The production assistants were bringing in trays of carbohydrates. It was only 9:40 ... plenty of time to grab a sesame seed bagel and dollop it with a gob of cream cheese.

I was reaching for a plate when a semi-familiar voice said, "Is this the home of The Simpsons?" I turned and walking into the room was Phil Hartman! I had read his name in the List of Characters and was told that he was going to be there, so that was not really a surprise. What really was a surprise was to ac-

tually have him walk in on me, unannounced. And . . . we were alone! All of a sudden my heart-rate kicked up to about 120 b.p.m.—I hoped I wasn't turning some unattractive shade of splotchy-red. Hopefully, all those years of aerobics were about to pay off and I wouldn't drop dead as I stepped over to say "hello" to the "funny man." I don't know what I was so freaked out about!

Clean-cut and unassuming, he had such a casual, no-nonsense way about him. It was that quality that we all find so hilarious, his delightful ability to poke fun at himself and at life, with a tongue-in-cheek attitude comparable to, say, Tim Conway or Mel Brooks or Carol Burnett. I had been a big fan of his ever since I had seen him as Kap'n Karl on The Pee-Wee Herman Show, *over-the-top but grounded in reality. Now, that takes talent. I don't know that anyone knows just exactly what it is that makes us laugh. But I believe that unless there is a certain honesty and a heightened reality, you ain't got bupkus! Phil has that magic. It's the* well-deserved *pie-in-the-face that makes you want to keep on watching. Leave us not forget his work on* Saturday Night Live *. . . Bill Clinton—ha! And his Ted Kennedy! He had always been hilarious and he was hilarious today, standing there grinning at me, and all he said was, "Is this the home of* The Simpsons?*"*

I started over toward him. Breathe, Nancy, I told myself. (I think I share this absurd quality with many: Faced with any funny man, I try to act very casual, but my heart thuds away while my mind desperately gropes for something clever to say.) Hey, Nance, I joked to myself, trying to calm my racing heart, if you can keep this up for another twenty minutes you'll burn off the cream cheese at Phil's expense. Hah, hah! Not funny. I thought— You're funny. You'll think of something funny to say!

I am not a comedienne. I love to tell stories, but I am horrible at telling jokes. Phil must be the life of the party. This guy must have everyone in stitches around the punch bowl. I would just stand back and enjoy the show. My mind spun at the thought of a competition or a talent show, where I'd be expected to do some sort of stand-up routine . . . I would be a nervous wreck!

So, he stood there, his eyebrow raised and I was in awe. "Awe," definition-wise, contains a certain element of fear. It isn't just a reverence or a respect. There is a little dread and wonder thrown in at no extra charge. So when Phil entered the room, the feeling that overwhelmed me, sending my heart into the strato-sphere, was awe.

Omygod! Call 911! The pressure. I don't know if Phil thought I was wiping cream cheese onto the napkin or if he re-alized that my palms were sopping. I guess my palms were just as excited to meet Phil as I was! Now, why didn't I just say that? That's funny. Isn't it? Just be cool, Nancy, I kept telling myself.

Walking over to him, moist hand extended, I said, "Yeah, The Simpsons. You got that right. I'm Nancy Cartwright. I'm a big fan of yours."

His face suddenly brightened. "Oh, you're the kid, aren't you?"

Interesting. He didn't ask me if I was Bart. He asked me if I was "the kid"! I didn't for one second think he didn't know Bart's name. It was a term of respect. "Kid." I was now classified with all the other great "Kids": Billy, Opie, Andy Hardy, Jackie Cooper, Macauley Culkin, Dennis the Menace. I liked him instantly. When you meet Phil, you want to be his best friend.

He was in today to play the character of Lionel Hutz, Springfield's most prominent shyster. He suddenly took on the whole persona of an attorney, standing there with his back perfectly straight, briefcase in hand.

He went on, "I'm a big fan too."

My heart began to ease up: 120, 118, 115, 110 . . . Mustering up my best Bart, I replied, "No way, man!"

He had a laugh. Score again! Ooops! 115, 133, 137 . . . The pressure is back. Funny once, must . . . be funny . . . always!

I fumbled forward. "Wow, it is so cool you're on our show."

Again, à la Lionel Hutz, "Yeah, well . . . someone's got to do it."

This time, I had the laugh. The ice was officially broken and I was able to breathe. He didn't expect me to keep this up. He didn't need me to be funny. Then he did a "change-up" that took me off-guard again. He dropped Lionel and the character's shysterishness (Say that fast three times!) vanished. He just looked me square in the eyes and I got the straight-poop: the sound of Phil.

"So, how many people show up for the records?"

"Well, because you're here, it'll probably be everyone on the whole lot."

He was taken aback, the fear I had felt showing momentarily in his face! Nancy to the rescue! "I'm just kidding. Actually, it starts out pretty full, with all the actors, writers, producers, their *assistants, the production assistants, and no kidding, there will probably be a few people who heard you were coming that wouldn't typically be here."*

Lionel resurfaced. And Phil said, with his classic expression, one eyebrow lifted, "Rupert?" [Rupert, as in "Murdoch," the Monarch of Fox News Corporation.]

"Yeah, right," I said laughing.

"Just checking. Gotta make sure the batteries in my tape recorder are still working. I'm wired, you know."

Pure Phil. What a cool guy.

Some Enchanted Beginning

I **was ten years old and pregnant, gestating my first-born daughter, Lucy,** and her animated twin brother, that infamous imp of Satan, Bart. It was the fall of 1989, the calm before the prime-time storm that I knew was coming, anticipation growing daily along with my waistline. It could have been a quiet oasis for me after completing our last Tracey Ullman short on Monday, October 24, at six in the evening. Matt and the crew of writers, producers and directors ran off to slave around the clock on the big gamble— writing, drawing, inventing the wheel of Springfield—but I could just take it easy and enjoy the thought of "my own personal production." I could take some time off . . . Yeah, right! Are you kidding?

You can imagine the impact this had on me—and I'm not

talking the motherhood part. I was about to be thrown into the world of *prime-time television*! Mind you, I had been making quite a comfortable living doing voice-overs for nearly eight years when *The Simpsons* went into its original slot at 8:30 on Sundays, right after *Married With Children*. The big difference was that now the audience was going to consist of not only kids, teens, young adults, college students, singles, married-with-children couples, married-with-no-children couples, middle-aged folks, and senior citizens, but also the parents of the kids, the parents of the parents of the kids, the kidless parents and parents who aren't kidding anybody! We're talking *millions and millions* of people! This was so cool.

The fashion-statement circa 1989 was spandex, oversized men's shirts and sandals. As maternity fashion goes, there might be a worse look, but I can't conjure anything up. I was into "Jane Fonda's Workout Record for Pregnancy, Birth and Recovery," doing dive squats and pelvic aligners. I was also going to see movies like *Milo and Otis* because I had heard that it had babies in it. Unfortunately, at every movie that I went to see that summer I ended up falling asleep about fifteen minutes into it. When I awoke, the idea that I was pregnant for the first time was amazing enough, but that I might be carrying a "Bart" inside me was more than I could handle. I remember rubbing my slowly expanding belly and saying, "Please don't be Bart. Please don't be Bart." After all, the only Bart I knew, the one from the bumpers, only had one side—and it wasn't good.

About a year earlier, I had met this great guy, Murph, through a mutual friend of ours, Dave Tourjé. He told me all about Murph and told Murph all about me. One day, my birthday, Dave and I were together and who should show up but this kinda cute-lookin' guy with twinkly eyes and a beard. He squared my shoulders and gave me a big kiss right on the center of my forehead. "Happy birthday, Nancy!" he twinkled. "Thank you. Who are you?" I squeaked. "Murph," he smurfed. I got a little flushed and needed to go get a drink of water. We went out the next night and two days later he moved in. What can I say? I am a sucker for a kiss. Two months later, we were married. See, I was just taking it easy.

When I met Murph he didn't even own a TV. He had no idea who Traccy Ullman was. It was through our relationship that I introduced Murph to the "magic of animation." He became a fast fan and any actor would love to have him in the audience. When he finds something funny, whether on the big or little screen, he laughs so hard and so completely that you can't help but laugh with him. I take him with me all the time. He's my own personal laugh track.

The first *Simpsons* half-hour script I ever saw was "Some Enchanted Evening" by Matt Groening and Sam Simon. Sam had worked with Jim Brooks on *Taxi*. Animation was a whole new deal for him. The script arrived on Saturday, May 6, 1989, at 1:30 *in the morning!* I was fast asleep, as was the entire household: hubby, two dogs and "baby on board." But shortly after Murph ambled down the sixty-seven steps that led to our front gate and stumbled back up again, he suggested that I tell whoever was in charge of delivery that they might consider just leaving it in the mailbox. I did and they have ever since. I proceeded to open the envelope. It was practically vacuum sealed with clear industrial tape in a gray oversized envelope. "Wow," I thought, "this must be some special script to be sealed in such a secure manner." I obviously had no idea what was to come! I grabbed the nearest sharp instrument and hungrily ripped it open to see who was who and what was what. To my surprise, the "family" had not only increased in size, but so had my participation. I was still Bart (whew!) and I would also be introducing Bubbles the Elf, one of a whole clan of elves including Moldy, Yendor and Doofy. Bubbles would reappear in *The Happy Little Elves*, Lisa's favorite show, but the others would fade into the forest.

This being the very first script *ever*, I was really curious as to how the show would transform itself from the little bumpers to a fully fleshed-out sitcom. In *The Tracey Ullman Show*, you got the "Basic Bart." He was very sarcastic, full of wit and wry with plenty of room for charm. At the time, it didn't occur to me that Bart could be anything but a little brat. But, moving into prime time, I knew that this meant there would be the possibility of finding that there was more to the little guy than we already knew.

At one point in the script, Bart is attempting to knock out the baby-sitter but has his fingers caught in a bowling ball. He looks up at Mrs. Botz and says, sheepishly, "I wish I could somehow convey to you how truly sorry I am." And this is done with total sincerity. This was good. This was a first. I let out a long, deep sigh of relief. It was clear that we would establish interesting, diverse and controversial characters. But would we have any problem making the leap into prime time? That question wouldn't be answered for almost a year.

I was absolutely astounded at the humor. Having already done forty-eight bumpers, Homer, Marge and Lisa were very clear to me. But who was Dr. Marvin Monroe? Moe? Barney? A lot of characters were not assigned yet. Who would play these parts? Did my fellow cast members, alone in their respective living or bedrooms, have the same curiosities?

That was one of the longest weekends ever. I was so excited. I could hardly wait to see Dan, Julie and Yeardley again. It had been nearly seven months and so much had happened in the meantime—and I had the stretch marks to prove it! I wanted to snatch up the phone and call them. I wanted to know what they were thinking. Did they like the script? Did they think it would work in prime time? Did they think their character and this family would develop?

Finally, the day arrived. I walked into the conference room above the soundstage where Tracey did her show. It was typical of most conference rooms at any studio: big, cold and plenty of fluorescent lighting. Fruit, bagels, coffee and orange juice and we were all set. I quickly scanned the joint, searching for someone I knew. I recognized Sam Simon and went up to him. He had been at a couple of our recording sessions, so he wasn't a total stranger. He seemed a little anxious—signs of "opening night jitters"—totally appropriate for the co-writer to have before hearing his script read for the first time. I told him how excited I was but he wasn't sure how the show was going to go over. I said to him, "Are you kidding? There isn't anything like this!" One thing I am never accused of is "being shy."

Matt was walking our way and I grabbed his arm. He smiled and gave me a hug. "How are you doing?" I asked. He smiled and said, "Fine," but I couldn't help but wonder if he really meant it. Here is the guy who established himself as an underground cartoonist, about to enter the fray of network prime-time broadcasting. He was a little harder to read. This was all so new to him, working with the whole lot of us. I wondered what was going on inside his mind. Was he agonizing inside? Did he sleep last night? This was the very beginning of something totally new, something never done before. And he was "The Man"! It was his little gem that initiated this whole party. The other cast members seemed to take it all in stride.

I looked over at Yeardley, who was chatting with Jim Brooks. She's a little younger than myself and has the face of a perennial teenager. I wondered if she felt as I did—high hopes and anticipation. At the time, she looked like she didn't have a care in the world. Julie was chatting away with one of the assistants. Actors are experts at hiding their feelings, or at least disguising them so as to not reveal too much. But with Julie, what you see is what you get. She is a straightforward and simple lady. I don't think she was losing sleep over this job. Scanning further, Dan was talking to Matt. Don't know what they were talking about, but from the look on Dan's face, it was clear that he too was having a good time and taking it all with ease. I had heard that because Julie and Dan were regulars on *The Tracey Ullman Show* they had been specifically asked to do the bumpers. That might have explained their remarkably calm state. Yeardley and I, on the other hand, had to audition, which puts a little added "ooomph" in the job . . . perhaps a little more at stake, but maybe not.

June Foray was there. I knew her from a few years ago. She is a voice-over veteran and pioneer in the industry and has given us hours of pleasure creating voices on *The Bullwinkle Show* and

The Sylvester and Tweetie Show. She was to be one of our supporting players. Her little old lady receptionist ("Rubber Baby Buggy Bumper Baby-sitting Service. May I help you?") might remind you of a certain Granny that was big with the Warner Bros. 'toons of not-so-long-ago. And she also piped out the voice of an elf that might remind you of a certain squirrel who has the same middle initial as Homer and Bart—Rocky J. (That's "J" as in Jay Ward, creator/father of the moose and the squirrel.)

There were lots of other folks, some actors but mostly staff. I made my rounds and got the consensus of the room. They were all very pleased to be there. There was a lot of social pitter-patter, not unlike a cocktail party, sans the hard beverages. But underneath it all lurked the anticipation of big surprise—perhaps Rupert would burst from a cake at any moment? It was time to start our very first table-read.

We read "Some Enchanted Evening" on May 8, 1989. With this first script, we began the tradition of meeting to do what is arguably the most exciting aspect of the production itself: the cast read-through. It was apparent that the whole cast wasn't fully assembled as there were many characters listed with no assignment next to them. The "family" was there, but the supporting players were still being considered.

I took one more glance around the room, looking at this curious group of talent. Clean-cut, well-groomed and not one "suit" in the whole bunch. I later found out that Fox was taking a back seat to the entire production so Matt, Sam and Jim could just run with it. Cool biz.

Let the read begin! " 'Some Enchanted Evening' by Matt

Groening and Sam Simon. Act One. Fade in: Exterior Simpson house—early morning." Julie had the first line of dialogue. Her squeaky-voiced Marge set the pace for the show. She finished her first line and got a lukewarm response. Uh-oh. We go on. She says her next line. Still no laugh. But, not to worry. It wasn't supposed to be funny. Then she says to baby Maggie, "Oh, I dread the day when you realize you're a separate human being." First laugh. Big laugh. Good deal. We go on more. A few chortles here and there, but no great response. One page goes by. Nothing. Another page. Still no laugh. Then on page five, Bart goes to the window to see the school bus. He calls out, "Hey, cool your jets, man. We're comin'!" Another great response. Good deal again.

This was all so new to each of us. We were going along just fine. It was wonderful to actually tell a whole story, instead of just a little snippet; and it all began to unfold as we continued the read. When a line would get a laugh, I'd look up and catch Matt's eye. He was laughing too. And when the next line produced another laugh, same thing, each of us catching each other mid-laugh. This was good.

We continued. Several pages went by with no laughs. Uh-oh . . . we got trouble in River City. A forced laugh every now and then. Then an honest laugh, then another and another until slowly, the cold room began to warm up with each one. The script was sounding pretty darn good. It really hit me in Marge's scene with therapist Dr. Marvin Monroe. She is upset because she feels "trapped in a loveless sham of a marriage." Monroe suggests she leave her husband.

Marge: Leave Homer?

Dr. Monroe: Please. Don't use his real name.

Marge: Leave Pedro?

It brought the house down. It was the first time that the whole room was laughing together, like a family of our own, enjoying this soon-to-be-public inside joke.

It was as if the entire room let out a huge sigh. It was as if we all knew the possibility was there, even though a certain "uncertainty" remained hiding in the corner. When we started, chairs were pulled in tight to the table. Now a few of them were pushed back a little more comfortably. Our eyes met, at home in the humor. And the laughter that was at one time forced was now coming from a place of honest appreciation and delight, especially from one end of the table.

Jim Brooks has always had one of those laughs that could convince you the phone book was funny. It's not that he was faking it, his laugh is so genuine, so free, honest, that it made it okay to just kick back and enjoy the ride. I don't know about the others, but whenever I heard Jim laugh, I knew that everything was A-OK.

The whole time we were recording *The Tracey Ullman Show* I had only met him once. He never came to any of the recording sessions, and we never had any other business that meant we would run into each other. The show was running smoothly, and I just supposed that Jim had other things a little more demanding than sweating it out in an already overly crowded sweatbox. I knew him only as one of the creative talents behind some of my favorites: from television, *The Mary Tyler Moore Show, Taxi, Rhoda* and *Lou Grant* and the feature films *Terms of Endearment, Broadcast News* and *Big.* As far as I was concerned, James L. Brooks was a god.

During the bumper year before we went half-hour, he was in preproduction on the film *War of the Roses.* Now that I know his work ethic, the man was undoubtedly immersed in it. For now, listening to his laugh, he brought a smile to my heart.

We finished the read with a unanimous "Aaaaaah!" The sigh of relief that I sensed earlier was now being vocalized for all to hear. A light round of applause, and we were done.

I glanced over at Matt, who was just starting to stand up. Jim leaned over and whispered something to him, pointing out some line in the script. Now they were both down in their seats again and Jim's arms were flying as he was describing some moment. Matt was nodding his head and taking a note. Then Matt said something, eliciting Jim's contagious laugh. It resounded through the entire room, driving all ghosts of doubt away. They both looked like they knew what they needed to do.

The first record took place the next day, but not at Fox. We met at 9:30 at Todd-AO, a recording facility in Hollywood. I don't know what got into me, but somehow I thought that because we were now going to be doing a prime-time show that we would actually get to work in a *real* studio *on the Fox lot!* How presumptuous. It's not that Todd-AO is a crummy facility. It isn't. In fact, it is one of the nicer ones in town. They had several different studios set up for postproduction and I was directed to the allotted space. I walked in and was greeted by the engineer and the rest of the gang. It was nice, but it still wasn't "home."

The script had been rewritten overnight and I did not receive a fresh copy until I got to the studio in the morning. That must have been an interesting night for the writers! Man, they knocked out a new script in less than twenty-four hours. I was impressed. The changes were subtle, but the whole thing had been tightened. There was no more "dead wood."

We got ourselves settled in and started to work. I thought, Oh, this will be a piece o' cake. I'll be out of here in time for a late lunch. Boy, was I wrong! We worked until *nine* that night! What were they thinking? All afternoon I kept saying to myself, Why is it taking so long to record fifteen minutes of dialogue?

We stood at our stands and got our scripts ready. We did a mike check, making sure that the mike was close enough to our faces so the sound would be clear and consistent. "Okay, let's go. Act One, Scene One, Take one. Action." The first scene was about six pages long. Most of the actors had already set up their pages on the stand in consecutive order, but a few just had their whole script plopped on it. We started the scene, but at the bottom of page one, pages had to turn and they wouldn't stay open and actors had to hold their scripts and it was all a little confusing, not to mention *noisy!* "Cut. You guys need to open up your scripts and lay them out on the stands." How embarrassing. I knew this but I didn't want to be a know-it-all, so I kept my mouth shut. Coming from all different backgrounds, not everyone knew how to lay out their scripts. (All that training as a Little Pony and Glo-Friend was beginning to kick in. Nifty.)

Okay. We got that stand-thing handled, so we moved on. "Okay. Act One. Scene One. Take two. Action." And we were off, again. This time we made it to about page four, when all of a sudden a couple pages from some stands lightly cascaded to the floor. They wafted downward, making just enough noise for those extremely sensitive microphones to pick it up. "Cut. You have to hold your pages." I couldn't hold back any longer. Stepping forward, Miss-Know-It-All, *moi*: "I know, but there are two more pages in this scene and not enough room on the stand. One way or another, it is going to make noise."

This "comedy of errors" continued into the afternoon. Stomachs growled. Noses sneezed. Papers fell. It was a long day. We finally got coordinated on the narrow-stand debacle following a quick demo from Miss-Know-It-All and everyone was set. I started half-kidding, half-pestering our engineer, Brad Brock, on a weekly basis. "Hey, Brad, how about running down to K-Mart for some stand extenders." This kidding/pestering went on for two seasons! Much to our surprise and pleasure, on the first day of season number three, we had brand-new wooden script holders that sat right on top of the music stands, extending the width a good sixteen inches. *Triumph! Victory! Success!* I was exuberant. "Stand extenders! What a brilliant idea! Whoever thought of that should be given a huge bonus—maybe a new car, to extend her driving pleasure?!" Alas, the car never arrived . . . can't blame a gal for trying.

That first show was quite remarkable. It was a whole new deal for all of us and we all had quite a bit to learn. "Okay, you guys. That was good. Let's do it again. Roll tape. Act One. Scene One. Take three. And . . . action!" So we did it again. Perfect. Got it. "... and cut. Good. That was great. But let's do it one more time. Roll tape. Act One. Scene One. Take four. And . . . action!" Another perfect take. A few changes were added, no extra charge, by the actors, thank you very much. And we were feelin' fine until . . . "Great. That was funny. You guys are good. Let's just do one more . . . for protection." I don't think any of us knew just what exactly we were being "protected" from, but we launched into takes five, six, seven, eight, nine . . . I might have had my baby right there, good grief! Yes, it was a learning experience. Why all these takes? I bit my tongue, as did the other actors.

The truth is that we were just "finding our legs." Gracie Films had never produced a prime-time animated show before. In fact, no one had for ages. *The Flintstones* held the record, but there were others: *Top Cat, Jonny Quest, The Jetsons* and *Wait till Your Father Gets Home*. It had obviously been a long, long time. We were really reinventing the training wheel, balancing what we knew with what we didn't.

The following week we did the table-read in the Tracey Ullman conference room, but the record was changed from Todd-AO to the Darryl Zanuck ADR stage. *Now this is more like it!* We were home at last. (We would hang our hats here for the next ten years.) Great! Terrific! Wonderful! *Bull——!* The place was a dump! The carpet hadn't been replaced since they did postproduction on *Lifeboat* in 1940! The ceiling had nasty water stains, hinting at some sort of plumbing problem that I didn't even want to think about. And behind a mock wall was a whole storage area that was used for god-only-knows-what toxic horrors. The baby within gave me a kick. You got that right, sister. I reached into the storage-horror and doused the light that was on for some mysterious reason. Well, that was handled! I gazed in suppressed horror at my surroundings. So, this was it, the "Big Time."

It was a huge soundstage. We each had a stool and a music stand to hold our scripts—just as small as the ones over at Todd-AO, by the way. There was a take-it-easy area whose centerpiece was an old leather couch. Thankfully, it smelled like leather. This was a terrific spot for me to chill with my ever-expanding baby. Alongside the couch were a couple of comfy chairs that we could grab when we weren't in a scene. But the most popular "prop" was the Ping-Pong table. Julie, Dan and supporting actress, Pamela Hayden, pretty much dominated it. I would pick up a paddle every now and then. I am a firm believer in beginner's luck, and I figured that if I didn't play all that much then each time I did, I would be a beginner all over again! I usually had my face buried in some expectant mother book. The curiosity factor had me but good.

Although I never experienced any morning sickness, I do recall being able to fall asleep at a moment's notice. This proved very beneficial when I didn't happen to be in the scene we were recording. I would stretch out on that couch and the lights would go out. But as soon as I heard my name, I would hop up and waddle over to the mike. Ha! Everyone thought I was just "resting my eyes"! I sure had them fooled.

The Darryl Zanuck was way back in the most distant corner on the Fox lot, the facility farthest from the front gate. Even so, I'm sure it was more convenient for everyone, since the writers and the Gracie offices were all housed on the lot as well. The only problem we actors had was no parking. Basically we had to trek from the front of the lot to the soundstage until we had complained enough that we "earned" parking spots nearby. (Parking is no longer such a precious commodity on the lot since the success of *The Simpsons* has contributed to a whole makeover of the studio.)

The day of our first record in our official studio, I remember driving up to the security kiosk and waiting with the rest of the "guests" to enter at the front gate. I was checked by security, instructed where to go and proceeded to the nearby parking area. I was so thrilled that our little vignettes were now a full-fledged show that I would have parked at the beach. (Just kidding!) Actually, and you are sworn to secrecy here, when I realized that we were way the heck over there and yet we had to park way the heck over here, it didn't make sense to me. So, I just drove over to the soundstage and found a spot. I told the security guard that I was on a new show called *The Simpsons* and we were recording right in the basement. He seemed impressed—and I figured if I ever had any trouble I'd just look real pregnant. Anyway, I never had a problem. (By the by, this actually became quite a controversy for some of us, frustrating as parking can be. We were well into our third season and still gnashing our teeth over the parking issue.) My magic wand was striking up a real relationship with the parking guys. Plus I was pregnant with baby number two— hey, if you've got it, flaunt it! I always found that if you just talk to people with some respect they usually respond in kind. Once we were a bona-fide hit, I ended up giving my table-read script to the parking lot attendant because he was always so helpful to me. (And if you're reading this: Just don't go sellin' it! That is meant for *you*!)

Oh, Danny Boy...

► **AUGUST 13, 1990**

"Who wrote this shit?!" The words had echoed inside the office* of the Hollywood producer. *Not a particularly cordial opening line when one is trying to impress another; however, in this case, it worked like a charm. I could never do it and get away with it, or so I believe. I'm far too polite. If you're from Ohio you don't say the S-word . . . except when you drop the soap in the shower, and, since a Buckeye never showers with anyone, no one would ever know.*

Today's guest with the unmistakable voice, whose career launched on the strength of "Who wrote this shit?!," was in to do Herb, Homer's long-gone half-brother in Jeff Martin's "Oh Brother, Where Art Thou?" Okay, I admit it. Guilty as charged

. . . *I'm a fan.* One Flew Over the Cuckoo's Nest, Terms of Endearment, Jewel of the Nile, Wise Guys, Ruthless People, Tin Men, Throw Momma From the Train, Twins *and* Taxi.

I have heard the stories: how he worked as a hairdresser at his sister's beauty salon in New Jersey before he became an actor, and how he threw the pilot script for Taxi *on the audition table and yelled his now legendary critique. My hero.*

This morning, at the table-read, I had just filled my plate with assorted strawberries, kiwi, papaya and mango when Bonnie said to my backside, "Nancy, I want to introduce you to . . ." and I turned and practically knocked over **Danny DeVito!** *all four feet, eleven inches of him, with my towering stature of five foot, one inch. How embarrassing! My fault. Sorry about that, Danny.*

Mr. DeVito, but I'll call him "Danny" since we have now worked together, had to get in and out fast because he was off to another appointment. We focused on recording his scenes only. I stood directly across the room from him, which was great because I got to see the man in action! I was secretly hoping that he would find fault with the script, not that it wasn't top-notch, but just to see him slam it down and burst a vein! I always loved his tirades as Louie DePalma. His tyrannical taxi dispatcher will always stand out as one of the great characters of television.

Most people think it doesn't take a lot of "acting" to do a voice-over well, but witnessing Danny would change your mind permanently on that consideration. He threw his body and soul into it. In an early scene, Herb is being introduced to the Simpson family. Homer snatches baby Maggie from Marge and tosses her to Herb. Dan Castellaneta mimed throwing "the bundle" and at just the right moment Danny "caught" the baby and took a big whiff, saying, "God, that new baby smell . . ."

Wes Archer, the animation director, was there and he madly scribbled, capturing some of Danny's attitudes, gestures and facial expressions as he performed. Wes was having a ball, his face intense, his hand occasionally running a sweaty palm through his mop, his eyes shining, just trying to keep up with the gyrations of Danny. By the end of the session, Wes's hair, which had started out as a mass of curls, needed some major reconstruction, not that he would notice. He was so focused on this rare treat—sketching Danny—he wouldn't have noticed if his pencil caught on fire.

I watched Danny, wondering what his life must be like. He isn't your average-looking Joe. Clearly, his voice is not the first thing you notice about him. I wondered what it would be like to be Danny DeVito. Going to a mall? A movie? Sunglasses wouldn't be much of a disguise.

In another scene, Herb tells Homer and the rest of the Simpson family to "[make] yourselves at home. . . . We have a tennis court, a swimming pool, a screening room . . ." This was obviously written with Danny in mind as I have no doubt that he actually has the aforementioned amenities in real life. (I'm presently living in a three-bedroom house with a stunning view of the freeway and our screening room is a VCR and poof chair.) He has earned his right to stand tall, and it wouldn't have shocked me to see him spew attitude all over us if he wanted to. But he's a hard worker and he concentrated on the job, his arms flying, his hair pointing in more directions than a sundial.

As the episode came to its climax, we discovered that all the material things in the world don't mean as much to Herb as being with family. Somehow I just get the feeling that this part was tailor-made with Danny, the family man, in mind. And it was the "baby toss" moment that gave him away.

Lady, That Ain't No Gutterball!

Some of the names that scroll by in the current postshow credits weren't on board in the first couple shows. As you can imagine, casting was a "work-in-progress"—or at least until Jim, Matt and Sam were satisfied that they had put together the best ensemble they could. God only knows how these decisions were made and He ain't talkin'. As they were getting us organized as a family, and we were getting synchronized as a cast, the eventual ensemble was sorted out. Harry Shearer and Hank Azaria, names that we share lead credit with now, both came in during the first season.

Harry was not at the original table read. When he finally did show up I immediately recognized him from his HBO one-man special. He once told me, in regard to work in this town, "You gotta keep 'em guessin'." And that he does.

Hank was originally brought in to be a supporting player and just seemed like a "regular guy" to me. He was very professional, but chimed in with some funny ad-libs and quips every now and then. The thing about Hank that I most remember is that he started out so unassuming and then, little by little, his abilities were revealed and his contributions to the show escalated. Starting out as just Moe, he was then given more and more characters until one day it occurred to me just how talented this guy was. Eventually, he and Yeardley were doing double-duty being on *Herman's Head* together. It was after that show was canceled that I realized Hank was going to be our breakaway star. And in a way, he is. His career has just skyrocketed and he has leaped into a whole new echelon because of his good work and great personality. His work in the films *Quiz Show* and *The Birdcage* and the TV movie *Tuesdays with Morrie* have earned him his good reputation. By the end of the first season we would have the whole team in place.

I knew Pamela Hayden and was aware of her talent, but did not know she had such a versatile range. She was cast as Milhouse right from the start, but also had the chops to make a totally different sound to play older characters. She has always been a very private person and someone who has a keen ability to observe what is going on before making any comments. It wasn't until years into the show that she and I got to talking and she told me that she was working on a one-woman show. This surprised me because I had always believed her to be too private to do something like that. But she would bring in her rough copies and diligently work on them in between takes and sure enough, one day she brought in invitations to her show. I went to see it and I was blown away! I learned so much about her—much more than she lets anyone in on at the records. Art has a tendency to do that.

And then there is Tress MacNeille, who, to me, is one of the most underacknowledged voice-over talents in the industry. She was brought in at the very end of season one, so it wasn't until that second season that we got to see her fully in action. She has one of the most facile voices around. From little kids to teens to adults to seniors, from girls to boys, she does it all. She can be an announcer, an executive, a spoiled brat, a ten-year-old Albanian spy, Lisa's girlfriend, a thug like Dolph and then switch over with ease to Skinner's mother. She does what it would normally take ten actresses to do. She is quiet and keeps to herself, diligently working in the background—a total pro.

Let us not forget Maggie Roswell, who came from a background that included many guest-star appearances on *M*A*S*H, Happy Days, Quantum Leap, Murphy Brown* and some animated shows. She was only in four of our first thirteen episodes, playing supporting parts. She became a regular cast member about halfway into our second season on "Dead Putting Society," with the introductions of both Maude Flanders and Helen Lovejoy. Maggie has been blessed with a skill in creating one of the hardest things to create: the "normal sound," whatever that is. So she can easily slip into the gal next door or any number of assorted reporters, medical students, jury members, accountants, scientists and moms. A contract dispute led to her departure as well as to the unfortunate demise of Maudie Flanders.

Although we don't see her face around Springfield much,

Russi Taylor has been with us sporadically since the first season. She has put her "voice-print" on Sherry/Terry, Uter and Martin, and like a fingerprint, each one is original. She comes from an extensive voice-over background, creating the voices for Strawberry Shortcake, Baby Gonzo in *The Muppet Babies*, Huey, Dewey and Louie in *Ducktales*, and Pebbles Flintstone as a teen and as a baby. But the most recognizable voice she does is that of Minnie Mouse. She has been "the official voice of Minnie" since 1986, when she went to work with Wayne Allwine, the voice of Mickey. This is the gig that keeps both Russi and Wayne hoppin' from coast to coast. But that's okay because, like Lucy and Ricky or Blondie and Dagwood, Russi and Wayne eventually tied the knot—nice to keep it all in the family!

We don't see nearly enough of Marcia Wallace, who is a celebrity in her own right, establishing one of the most memorable character parts as Carol Kester Bondurant on *Newhart*. That wry-in-your-eye wit carries over well as Mrs. Krabappel. She pops in and out semiregularly, when she isn't performing on television or stage somewhere or on another lecture tour. In her spare time, besides raising her son, she has written her memoirs.

The newest member to *The Simpsons* cast is Karl Wiedergott. He has quite an extensive theater and independent film history. He joined us a couple years ago to fill in at the table-read when Hank, Harry or Dan were off on another job. Pamela, Tress and Maggie were always there to do an occasional Marge, Bart or Lisa, but we never had a guy there to fill in for our guys. They will also fill in at the recording, but this is done as a temp track, to be rerecorded with the regular cast member at a later time. In addition to filling in with complete style, Karl does a pretty mean Jimmy Carter and does a fair amount of waiters, lawyers, doctors and other assorted extras.

THE keynote of evolution is striking when you review the episodes from year one. Dan's main character, Homer, evolved, if you will, into the strong, three-dimensional character we love to shake our heads at. What Dan had created in the shorts was fine for a grumpy-burp-of-a-guy who choked his son to wind down, but it had a limited range. He realized quickly, when confronted with scenes that asked for more emotion—"My beer! My beer! My precious beer!"—that the vocal placement wasn't working. By extending his pitch, both high and low, he was able to create more flexibility and thus add to the humor of the character. So the Walter Matthau sound evolved into the Homer we know and love today!

It happened gradually during the first season, but not always smoothly. Taking a look at the shows in order you would be hardpressed to spot exactly where and when the change actually took place, and for a while it seemed that Homer was a bit schizo. At first he'd sound like Matthau and then like the Homer we know, and then back and forth. But most assuredly by the end of that first year, Dan had worked out the mechanics of Homer's voice.

Julie's Marge also evolved a bit. When we first started, Marge's voice was pitched a bit higher and also had a very "wavy" sound to it. Personality-wise, Marge was a little ditzier at first, but as that first season rolled on, she became more stable and so did her voice.

One complete change was to Mr. Burns's voice. It meta-morphosed into a completely older sound. Harry had originally pitched the tyrant's voice to infuse Burns with the energy of a younger man. By the end of the first season, he had evolved into the rotten, avaricious coot we have come to know and love. (Burns, not Harry.)

Another actor originally voiced Moe, but Hank Azaria was brought in by the fourth show, "There's No Disgrace Like Home." Moe, at that time, wasn't exactly the same guy either in voice or look. Hank took him into more gravel, a more mature sound, and Moe "responded" to Hank's characterization over a couple epi-sodes. The animation followed Hank's lead and Moe's jet black hair aged a bit with a modest touch of gray, adding a little pepper to his already salty character.

IT didn't take long to settle into a groove. We were all working actors and quickly got used to a schedule that left a lot of freedom to do other things. Ten o'clock on Thursday mornings for the one-hour reading and ten to six on Mondays to do the record. A couple more hours for postproduction, and that was about it.

A group, depending on how long it remains together, will have interpersonal dynamics that tend to shift and change. Once you get familiar with one another's idiosyncrasies, desires, work habits, etc. the energies sort of . . . sort themselves out. I have never really considered *The Simpsons* ensemble as a "group" in the traditional sense of the word. We don't make decisions to-gether, don't do much together, don't support one another like a family would. We'll go see a one-man show—"Great work,

Dan!"—but we don't go as a group. We'll listen to "What Did You Do On Your Summer Vacation" stories, but it doesn't tend to go deeper. The nature of working on this show is not particularly conducive to an in-depth sort of a relationship. We are together, really, when you look at it, barely one day a week for a couple of weeks, then we have a week or even two off. There isn't a whole lot of time to really get into any kind of significant conversation. We are all very much into our own worlds and yet some of us (more than others) are a little more supportive by going to the plays, shows, performances of another. We don't "share" what else we are working on and we never have. Sometimes someone might ask, "So, what else are you doing?" But that is rare.

Earlier on, when we used to be there the whole day and have to take a lunch break, a group of us would go off to the commissary. Julie's folks live nearby so she would always go have lunch at their house. Always. And Harry just never wanted to join us. Never. Tress would often bring her own lunch or go off to meet someone. But Dan, Yeardley, Pamela, Maggie, Hank and I would go off with Louise, the script supervisor, and eat on "the good side" or "the cheap side."

I guess this is a little sad, to me at least. There's a part of me that would like to say that we are "best friends," that we hang out together and even socialize outside of the show. But that just isn't true. For the most part, there is mutual respect and a general understanding that we are all professionals and we are together on this great gig. We have seen each other take on new personal challenges, a couple of babies, several weddings, several more divorces, a new series, lots of movies, guest appearances and other opportunities. It's no one's fault, really. It just makes me wonder what it might have been. But I don't know that it would have been possible to create a tighter group, given the dynamic of this particular "family." "Being busy" can make ten years slip by in a blink.

Any nerves I felt in those early days were a direct result of being put on the spot, so to speak, to play certain characters. Unlike every other animated show that I have been on, where I would get a chance to work on and make choices regarding a particular character, on *The Simpsons*, as new characters were introduced, there weren't "auditions." We just came up with them on our own prior to the cast read. I find this extraordinary. This is a novel approach to casting: just assign the actors the parts and let them work it out! On the one hand, it was great because there was a lot of freedom to come up with a new sound or a new attitude. Similar to improvisation, there is a certain amount of risk involved and when you score a hit, it's wonderful. But, on the other hand, it was a lot of pressure, creating a fully fleshed-out character with no input from the writer or show runner. I must say, "the boys" on the show really blow the girls out of the water in this area. Averaging twelve characters apiece, Dan, Hank and Harry still amaze me with how many voices they do!

It was always a treat and remains one of the highlights of the readings when new characters are introduced. Just how many ways can an actor change his voice? Accent, pitch, pacing, range, intention—it all comes into play. Sometimes it isn't even a very big change at all from your regular voice, but the attitude behind it makes all the difference in the world. For example, we were going to have a guest star play Frank Grimes in "Homer's Enemy"—remember him?—briefcase, sixties haircut, personalized pencils. Hank, at the table-read, just filling in, created such a beautifully crafted character, beautifully psychotic, that no one was used to replace him.

Another character vocally carved out by Tress MacNeille was "Belle" from the Maison Derriere. Her skills are plentiful, with a range comparable to that of "the boys." This character also was due to be celeb-voiced but Tress's performance at the table read couldn't be beat. In addition, she belted out all the vocals for Belle, making herself extremely difficult to be replaced. She is as award-winning as you can get.

Another performance that just killed me was by Maggie Roswell. She was substituting for a celebrity, who shall remain nameless. (These identity-less celebs are the unchosen few who have never walked the streets of Springfield.) This was the tour-de-force part of "Shary Bobbins." I am telling you, this is one of my all-time favorite episodes. The whole spin on this satire was so brilliantly crafted and Maggie's Shary is top-drawer. Listen to her on the CD *Songs in the Key of Springfield* and see that you don't agree. She has the attitude, the energy and especially the pipes to pull off the best Julie Andrews (oops, forgot—I wasn't going to name names!) ever to drop into a sleepy, little town—umbrella and all.

In "Bart the General," Nelson Muntz is first introduced. A good friend and multitalented actress of screen and voice, Dana Hill, was originally assigned to do the part. She was at the reading, yet the producers were still putting together this ensemble of players and, come Monday, at the recording, she was nowhere to be found and the part was assigned to me. I didn't have time to ask why and still don't have a clue. Quickly, I asked myself, "What does a bully sound like?" Well . . . what you hear is what you get. When I first uttered, "I'll get you after school, man!" I let out a sigh of relief when I got through the line and a double-sigh when it got a laugh. Haw-haw!

AN actor's challenges just don't go away. When asked, "What if you have a scene and you have to play two characters, what do you do? Talk to yourself?" Me? I keep my fingers crossed and keep breathing! "The boys" do this far more frequently than the women. This might be due to the fact that most of our lead characters happen to be men, or boys written by men, okay, just boys! It is absolutely fascinating to observe. Burns and Smithers are rarely without one another and Dan will have conversations with himself as Homer, Grampa, Barney and/or Krusty with one or more ancillary characters thrown in at no extra cost. To watch these actors doing multiple voices, in conversation with themselves, is a show that you wouldn't want to miss. It takes extreme concentration and the ability to change your whole personality in a millisecond. As actors, we have the ability to turn it on and turn it off. There just isn't enough time to use Method acting in voice-over work. You either got it or you ain't.

Challenges like the above didn't get to me in the first season. I had my Everest to climb in season ten with "Simpsons Bible Stories." These moments are either an actor's dream or an actor's nightmare—depending on whether or not you pull it off! I checked out the script. I had one line in Act One. Yawn! Three lines in Act Two. "Wow, I'm hardly in this show at all." Act Three . . . "Oh, my God. I am playing Bart, Nelson and Ralph . . . *for ten pages!*" "Challenge" definitely describes it, but perhaps a more accurate description might be . . . *crazy!* I crossed my vocal cords and jumped in.

The scene went on and on, and I went on and on. There was no time to think. There was no time to wonder. And to observe an actor change from one character to another means to watch his or her body and face take on a totally different look. For Bart, I remain very open, not much change from what I normally look like. But with Nelson, my brow furrows and I get a very angry look on my kisser. Poor guy—he could definitely use a little R and R. With Ralph, my eyes get huge and my eyebrows go way high. I get a sort of dopey-look on my face, making me look totally innocent. We don't think about what we look like when we do voice work, but the change in appearance is inevitable, since we really are becoming these characters.

By the time I finished my conversation with myself, I was a little shaken and a lot out of breath. Nelson tends to do that to me. He takes a lot of breath control. After the ten pages, the room burst into applause and I was totally taken aback. I looked up and Julie was giving me the thumbs up sign and you'd have to ask her, but I am pretty sure my face was a subtle shade of crimson. Nice surprise. When that read was over, I just made sure that I was Nancy Cartwright when I walked out of the room!

The rest of that first summer was spent recording the remaining twelve episodes of the season. As the months passed, my flat tummy began protruding. Because I am just over five feet tall, my pregnancy, at first, just looked like I was gaining a little weight. It wasn't until I was well into my seventh month that I actually looked pregnant. I grew as the show grew, taking shape within the walls of strange buildings filled with hunched-shouldered artists poring over character sketches that would one day be seen by the world.

While all this voice work was going on, clear on the other side of town, at Klasky Csupo, an animation studio in Hollywood, they were up to their chinless-chins with character design ideas, color samples and the start of a storyboard layout. It was clear that we weren't the only ones working our animated yellow butts off.

As you may imagine, doing animation is a costly and time-consuming process. In the very earliest stages of the show, the animators, Matt Groening, and Sam Simon, were all trying to figure out what worked and what didn't work. It was obvious that the transformation from the shorts to the show itself was a rough and demanding change. The characters were crudely drawn by Matt for *The Tracey Ullman Show* and originally the animators tried to maintain that look. But it was quickly discovered that the sharp angles and the very rigid artwork made it extremely difficult for them to duplicate precisely and in quantity. In fact, because of this, our very first recorded show, "Some Enchanted Evening," had to be completely reanimated. What a nightmare! All the work had to be redone as it was not the quality that Matt wanted to present. It took months to do over. In fact, because of the delay, this first recorded show aired as the *last* show of the first season!

I can imagine the animators endured many sleepless nights while trying to come up with exactly the right look for the show.

What they had to set up was a system to get the animators from Korea to duplicate exactly what our guys had designed. The characters had to be rounded out a bit, softened so they were easier to draw in bulk and in a timely fashion—and always in keeping with the original concept from Matt. Once it was set, that was it. The character designs were locked-in and have remained the same ever since. These funky, crude, yellow-skinned, chinless characters soon became the rage of all television.

Sometime toward the end of '89, word was out that our regular time slot was going to be Sunday nights at eight-thirty. We couldn't have been more pleased. Sunday nights mean "family" and that is a perfect time for the perfect family show! From my childhood, Sunday nights have always meant time to slow down, and time to take a bath early and watch *The Wonderful World of Disney*. It meant that the weekend was over and tomorrow was Monday, which meant back to school and homework. Sunday nights were the last vestiges of family-togetherness in this social-butterfly's life. But we only had that time slot for the first thirteen episodes.

Beginning in the fall of 1990, Fox, in a "creative ratings ploy," moved *The Simpsons* to Thursday nights, opposite *The Cosby Show*. If you ever have wanted to see a group of grown-up kids have a hissy fit, you should have seen us when that decision was made. Man, were we pissed, but we didn't have a whole lot of say in the matter. No one consulted us. No surveys were done. I was personally offended—how dare they threaten my "family time"! We held our own against the Huxtables, but it was a game that we were not interested in playing. Finally, in the fall of 1994, we were moved back to our original night, but this time at eight o'clock. Fox realized the power they had with *The Simpsons*, but this was just the beginning! Needless to say, we kids were thrilled! But I'm getting a little ahead of myself.

Just before we made our television debut, the producers decided that Christmas would be a great time to kick off the premiere episode. So, even though "Some Enchanted Evening" was the first show we recorded, it was "Simpsons Roasting on an Open Fire" that garnered all the attention.

This episode was actually the eighth show that we recorded. Much to our advantage, this gave us seven other shows in which to develop the look, continuity and sound of what was presented in that Christmas special. Consequently it was an impressive pilot.

There are a couple of interesting footnotes. This would be the first time America would see the Simpson family surrounded by a bevy of new characters, including: Principal Skinner, Mr. Largo, Patty and Selma, Ned Flanders, Mr. Smithers, Mr. Burns, Moe, Barney, Milhouse and, of course, Santa's Little Helper. (Or as he is sometimes referred to, Number Eight.) Ralph briefly appears in this episode, although actress Jo Ann Harris did his voice at the time. (It wasn't until much later, in the fall of '91, in "Bart, The Murderer," that I was officially assigned the voice of Ralph when he smiles and says, "I'm gonna eat chocolate 'til I barf.")

The episode's main plot centers on the Springfield Elementary School's annual Christmas pageant. It is here that we are introduced to "Prime-time Bart," and he does not disappoint. The traditional bratty boy who was already set up in Tracey's show is carried through here with Bart saying for the first time, "I'm Bart Simpson. Who the hell are you?" And the traditional chokehold that was established during the shorts is presented here as a perfect last note during the end credits. But there were new aspects to his character.

After working together for half a season, the writers had time to "flesh out" the characters, so to speak, making them more three-dimensional. Bart, in this first episode, has a couple of moments where he's more than a riff on *Dennis the Menace.*

Homer is picking up his check at the personnel office for working part-time as a Santa Claus. He is devastated, because after subtracting the Social Security, unemployment insurance, Santa training, costume purchase, beard rental and Christmas club, he is left with a total sum of $13. You hear for the first time that Bart really feels for his dad when he says, "Come on, Dad. Let's go home." I wrote a little direction to myself in pencil in the script that helps reinforce the further development of Bart. It says, "Saves his dignity." I definitely liked the direction we were going.

Marge was also more defined. Julie had been exploring just exactly where to place Marge's voice and by the eighth record she had really settled in on a very specific sound. She had far more emotional tones than just harping at Homer and the kids. Here she is presented as the real glue for this family. She has pride and integrity and you really feel that she loves Homer. The animators reinforced her good work in a quiet moment in the bedroom when they have Marge gently lay her hand upon Homer's. Sweet.

Homer still had a wee bit of the Walter Matthau sound to his voice, but he was leaning more to the sound that we are familiar with now. What you really get is the emotional range that Dan has, especially in the moment where he sees the empty jar that was supposed to hold all the family's Christmas money. He is up and down an emotional scale like a jumping bean. *"IT'S TRUE! THE JAR IS EMPTY! OH MY GOD! We're ruined. Christmas is canceled. NO PRESENTS FOR ANYONE!"*

No doubt about it, Yeardley's character had more of a developmental change than anyone else's. On the bumpers, she was pretty much like Bart and all Bart and Lisa did was bicker. But this first episode really establishes that Lisa has a mind of her own.

In the script, Homer and Bart have been gone all night long. Seeing as it is Christmas Eve, Patty's comment to Selma is the perfect put-down for the brother-in-law she can't stand: "It's so typical of the big doofus to spoil it all." Lisa interrupts with, "What, Aunt Patty?" Patty again with, "Nothing dear. I'm just trashing your father." And this is where Lisa shines. "Well, I wish you wouldn't because, aside from the fact that he has the same frailties as all human beings, he's the only father I have. Therefore, he is my model of manhood and my estimation of him will govern the prospects of my adult relationships. So I hope you bear in mind that any knock at him is a knock at me; and I am far too young to defend myself against such onslaughts." We love her—Yeardley and Lisa.

The most obvious evolution can be seen in the beautiful animation directed by David Silverman and Wes Archer. Of course, no one outside the inner workings of the show would know about the evolution itself. It just ended up looking very different—and very great.

I'm not sure if it was on this particular episode, but one of my personal favorite stories is one I had heard about that first year. Some artwork had been designed and sketched in pencil for approval. There were "creative differences" and both David and Wes were putting in some serious overtime to get the problems sorted out. They were behind in schedule and needed to get the artwork shipped overseas. In a heated moment of frustration and compassion, Wes picked up a two-inch thick stack of penciled artwork and was waving it around wildly. David, the less animated of the two, queried, "Wes, what are you doing?" And with that, Wes opened the window and tossed out the whole kit and caboodle! "It's shipped overseas! There it goes! Overseas!" Apparently he continued to "ship" the work "overseas" the rest of the evening. Rumor has it that one of the producers just happened to be driving by in her car and was the recipient of this animated confetti. Nothing scarier than seeing some of your own work "displayed" on your windshield! The artwork eventually developed beyond road kill and did make it to Korea, where the inking and painting of the cels takes place. (More on this later.) Eventually the transition from the harsh and sharp visuals in the shorts to the fully realized style that Matt insisted on for the half-hour show, the look we are so familiar with today, was completed. In "Simpsons Roasting on an Open Fire," I love the image of the magnified lens looking at Bart's tattoo. It's pure fun and just not expected. And at the end of Act One Homer feels helpless and is standing in the snow, all alone. The camera cuts to him and at just the right instant, he bows his head. It is a real sweet moment that breaks your heart—and an honest, sensitive touch that no other animation on prime-time television had even hinted at!

With this premiere episode, we also established the catch phrase that soon was silk-screened on one of the most sought-after T-shirts in America. Bart is strapped to a stainless steel gurney. He is staring into a ray-gun that is poised to laser off the "Moth—" tattoo. With all his justifiable angst and all his might, he screams out, "Ay caramba!" I don't recall learning this phrase in ninth grade Spanish, but I have no doubt that Bart has contributed in more than one way to culture—Spanish or otherwise.

While all the shows were outstanding, there are two episodes from that first season that really win my vote for best: "The Crepes of Wrath" and "Krusty Gets Busted." "Crepes" was the final show to be animated that year and "Krusty" just preceded it, so the look was clean as a hound's tooth by the time these episodes were produced.

"Crepes of Wrath" really puts you on an emotional rollercoaster. Bart is causing so many problems at school that he is shipped off to France as an exchange student. Principal Skinner and Homer have this hilarious moment when they are told that Bart wants to go. They "high-five" each other and the timing of the animation and the acting is spot-on. Wes Archer directed this episode with the flair and originality of a French chef at a five-star gourmet restaurant—with just a dash of directorial brilliance. When Bart is in France, the dialogue includes subtitles. The idea that a cartoon would include subtitles is hilarious in itself and the animators pulled it off brilliantly. Also, I love that there is an entirely new emotional aspect to Bart. The viewer is really moved when the French brutes insist that Bart sleep on the ground. Poor little guy, it tugs at your heartstrings. Later you feel great relief when Bart spontaneously begins to speak in French. It is one of my all-time favorite moments in the lifetime of the show. The challenge for *moi* is that I don't speak French! A dialect is one thing . . . conversational speaking is another! A French dialectician was hired to teach me the pronunciations. *Oui!* That was the easy part. Le problem was Bart's looooooooong monologue eliciting help from a *gendarme* (a policeman, for all you non–French speaking fans!). It is one intense piece of dialogue. *Sacre bleu!* In order for me to be able to put across exactly the frustration and intention that Bart was feeling at that moment, it wasn't good enough to just know how to pronounce the words. I had to know what I was saying when I was saying it . . . duh! This is where my speech and forensics background really came in handy. In order to marry the French with the understanding of the English, I wrote out how to pronounce the words using phonetics. (I had actually taken a class at Ohio University. Kudos to Dr. Gee for stressing the sĭg-nĭf'i-kans uv fa-nĕt'iks.) I just wrote out the dialogue phonetically just above the English version. It took a bit of eye-mouth coordination, but a couple passes through and it was just fine. Of course, anyone who wasn't there wouldn't know any different. As far as they were concerned, I am fluent in French. *Aaaah, les wondres de animation!*

In "Krusty Gets Busted," I was totally knocked out by the new camera angles that Brad Bird, the director, took on. I loved the moment when Homer searches for some ice cream at the Kwik-E-Mart and the camera is inside the cooler, looking up at Homer's face. "Mmmm . . . ice cream." Also, relevant to the times, there was a hilarious moment when Patty and Selma are bragging about their vacation. Cut to Selma taking a siesta, à la Madonna—complete with the "snow cone" bra. Very fun stuff. The character definition to get this across, both in the artwork and in the voice work, is superb. Kelsey Grammer absolutely astounded me with his rendition of a Cole Porter song, "Ev'ry Time We Say Goodbye." This was the first time we had the luxury of actually having the celebrity guest in the studio with us.

The fact that I was the size of the nuclear power plant in Springfield wasn't about to stop me from attending the premiere party at Barney's Bowlerama, a.k.a. Pickwick Bowl. I was soon to find out that *The Simpsons* throw the most incredible parties. From mini-golf, to bowling, to science museums, the theme is fun and games. They are *not* to be missed. It was December 17th, and I arrived with Murphy, proud hubby of giant wife. I had no idea what to wear to this momentous occasion. All I knew was I was as big as Montana and nowhere near feeling very pretty. I thought, "If I can't beat 'em, I'll join 'em." So, I had a friend design and sew me a white satin jump suit with a bright red nylon band around my swollen belly. It was perfect. I looked every bit like a bowling pin.

The party was well attended. Excitement bubbling in the air. There were monitors in every lane and several big screen TVs. I hardly knew a soul and it just amazed me how many people it took to do one show. There must have been 1,000 people there (give or take a few hundred) with at least one third of them actively involved with the show. I am still amazed at the number of artists *The Simpsons* has successfully employed over the years. Keeps the riffraff off the streets.

We partied on. I didn't last long, however, as my due date was a couple days—er, hours?—away. Never one to refuse a challenge when I see one, however, I wanted one more shot at a perfect 300. Hmm, it must have been that last gutterball in the first frame, because shortly after arriving home, my water broke and Lucy Mae was born.

Me at age ten—the day I won the speech contest with
"How the Camel Got His Hump."

Me in the final round of the National District
competition at Ohio University, taking first place.

Me doing the voice of "Lily Padd" at WING-radio with deejay Ken Warren.

My mentor, my friend, Daws Butler.

Another shot of Daws, voice of
Elroy Jetson, Yogi Bear,
Huckleberry Hound and others.

A treasured shot of Daws and me.

Here I am with my first animation "family": Sparky Marcus, the voice of Richie Rich, and Stan Jones, the voice of Mr. Rich. I was the voice of Gloria.

The last of my faithful car "Spud." May he rest in peace.

Lisa Freeman, Deena Freeman (not related) and me
in the ABC pilot *In Trouble*.

The King of Improv, Jonathan Winters.

Me in the lobster hat Jonathan
gave me as a memento.

Me in the title role of the CBS movie-of-the-week
Marian Rose White.

Playing sixteen-year-old Ethyl in Joe Dante's *Twilight Zone, the Movie.*

Opening night of my one-woman play, *In Search of Fellini,* October 27, 1995.

Storyboard panel being drawn by artist Brad Ableson.

ABOVE: Brad Ableson after working all night on storyboards.

RIGHT: Layout artist Norm Auble flips a series of key-pose drawings. Model sheets, a mirror used for facial-expression studies and other staff members over the cubicle wall can be seen in the background.

A typical animation drawing held over an animator's disc.

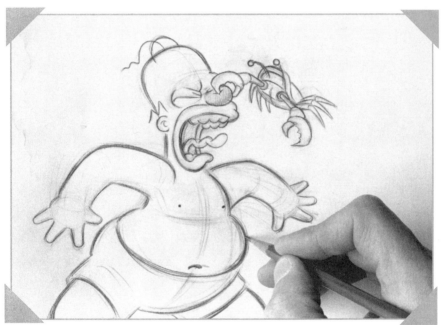

Layout pose of Homer with a crab being drawn by artist/director Mark Kirkland.

Photo by Mark Kirkland. Used by permission.

The final check: Larry Smith studies an animation pose before it's shipped overseas.

Photo by Mark Kirkland. Used by permission.

An animation crew view their own work for the first time.

Recording dialogue for Bart.

Julie, Dan, myself and Yeardley—but who'd ever know?!

Me at the Emmy Awards® in 1992.

Here we are getting our Simpsons star on the Hollywood Walk of Fame
on January 14, 2000: (from left) Yeardley Smith, Matt Groening,
Jim Brooks, me and Pamela Hayden.

Do the Bartman!

▶ **AUGUST 31, 1990**

S *o what do you give someone who already has everything? What do you* *buy for a guy who is worth an estimated $450 million? What kind of thing do you purchase for the oldest "boy" in the world? What sort of present do you give to the first solo artist to generate four Top-Ten hits on the* Billboard *charts on one album, seven top hits on another album and five number-one hits on yet another album? What do you give to a man who doesn't really want anything, except to be accepted? What do you give to Michael Jackson? It took days to figure out.*

Flashback to earlier this week. Yeardley and I were meeting with producer John Boylan at Lion's Share to find out what key we sang in. He also played some sample cuts from our new Simpsons CD, Simpsons Sing the Blues, *that had been recorded by some studio singers. Good singers. It was the first time I got to hear Yeardley's voice. Wow! So sweet and pure . . . just perfect for "God Bless the Child." Me? I'm okay, but Bart Rocks!*

We were jammin' to the sample of "Do the Bartman" when John leans over and says, "I won't be directing you on this one." "Oh, bummer!" I replied. "Yeah," he went on. "Some guy named Michael's gonna lead you." It took a few seconds for the penny to drop and my jaw quickly followed.

Michael?! I raced to the nearest mall. A set of sunglasses? A T-shirt? A nice tie? Jesus! Something more personal. I raced home and rummaged every closet. My trumpet? Never! That negligée? A family photo? I had to think of something. I don't know why, just had to. Then, as I dug deeper into my collection I heard the strangest thing. Little Lucy, all of nine months, got her finger in the string of a talking Bart doll and I heard my own altered voice say, "Eat my shorts." Problem solved. I have about ten of these dolls and besides the "shorts" line it voices about five other expressions that have been incorporated into our American vernacular. Pretty sad. The vernacular, not the doll. The doll is actually kinda cute. His proportions are very real and the hard plastic head is big and yellow and his eyes bug out. Very Bart. I figured this might be just the perfect gift for the guy who has everything.

Standing in the lobby, the front door opens and in he walks. He had on his sunglasses and was a little taller than I had imagined. Jim was right there and shook his hand and said a few things, welcoming him and all. Then, Michael turned to me. I had the doll behind my back because I wanted to surprise him. I had signed the doll's belly and written "Bart ♡ Michael" on the front of his T-shirt.

Just as we finished our greetings, I pulled the doll out from behind and handed it to him, saying, "This is from me to you."

He just about had a heart attack! His eyes lit up like a six-year-old's and he took it and hugged it. "Omygod, he really is a kid!"

He thanked me profusely and, from that moment on, I knew we were going to have a great time.

We went into the studio and began the rehearsal for "Do the Bartman." Michael was absolutely incredible. We had so much fun. It didn't take us very long at all because he knew exactly what he was doing. We started at the top and just ran through it a couple of times and he couldn't stop laughing. He absolutely loved Bart and when I spoke like him, Michael was delighted . . . like a kid at Christmas.

At one point in the song, there was plenty of room for ad-libbing. I went nuts. I added this one toward the end, "Eat your heart out, Michael," and he loved that! I hope it stays.

We finished and he gave me a copy and gave me a hug. And then I went out to the very cozy living room and had a little lunch.

Oh, and by the way, those dolls? I found them on sale at Toys "R" Us for $10 apiece. They retailed at $30. I snatched them all, it was such a deal. Hey, you never know when you might run into Michael Jackson.

Remembering Elizabeth

► MAY 28, 1992

I *couldn't help myself. I turned to Yeardley and said, "Dah-link! What*
do you think of my new bauble?!"

There was an unusual buzz in the air at our weekly recording
session this morning and it had nothing to do with pending con-
tract negotiations or the fact that there was talk about moving our
time slot again. These "vital topics" were now no more interesting
than Southern California weather. We didn't have much time for
any real conversation, even on a regular day. As soon as we would
get chatting and would reach the point of making a point, we'd
be interrupted with, "Dan, Nancy, Yeardley, Julie . . . you're
needed for Scene Five." Today's buzz of mellow morning mike
manipulation and warm-up exercises—like saying "unique–New

*York" three times fast, or "red-leather, yellow-leather"—were
eclipsed by the buzz saw of anticipation of "Hollywood Royalty."
(Caps are mine, quotation marks are mandatory.)*

*Eyes kept darting toward the entrance of the recording stu-
dio, that is, the "chambers" in which we were all kept in-waiting.
Even though we were all doing our best to look like we didn't
care, a stranger would have expected the Second Coming after
observing us for two minutes. You don't have to be starstruck in
this case. A supernova cannot be ignored.*

*Suddenly, between a sip of tea and a nibble of scone, in
walked what could only be called an entourage. They entered as
if with scepter and ball, with an air of those who precede great-
ness, as if the Grand Canyon were in tow. Like keepers at the
gates to a great mystery they came. The first man's head nearly
brushed the door frame; he had a hairline that started at his ears
and went right back around. His hunched, middle-aged frame was
outfitted in a color just shy of royal blue. But then again the whole
scene was just a little "off" anyway. He wore an expression of
perpetual surrender. Next came Mr. Hollywood, perfectly clothed
in a jet-black suit and brand-new, dazzlingly white Nikes. This
outfit is the tuxedo of Hollywood casual. Those shoes go for about
two bills and we all know it. The suit has a four-figure look. He's
dressed down, of course, taking it easy today, but one can only
go so easy in his position as attendant to The Queen. Right behind
him came a not-really-fat but short-and-stocky guy clutching a
woman's handbag. Let the show begin!*

I half expected Fellini to walk in next to set the scene, but these three pozzos were only the appetizer for the main course, who sauntered into our studio, bringing with her the faint scent of gardenias and fame.

A silence fell in The Queen's quarters, as if the universe were taking a long breath and then—in she strode, bedecked in a white pantsuit with a feather-boa collar, her big hair looking a little too coiffed, a diamond on the left-hand ring finger the size of Nebraska. She was a sight to behold. Makeup hardly describes what she does in the morning. When minks are as much a part of your wardrobe as socks, makeup is done by Maxfield Parrish.

I could feel my knee bending in supplication but fortunately the table was there to prevent that embarrassment. The icing on the diva cake was the little white pup that she snuggled close to her heart. I assume this Pekingese, Lhasa apso, or whatever, was toilet trained as there were no "oopsies" on her silk blouse. The feisty little pooch was not comfortable with the crowd, or maybe it was the perfume, but his mommy was compassionate, if not effusive in her sympathy as she attempted to calm him. "Look at all the nice people." Yes, as if a drumroll were sounding and trumpets blaring, the official voice of Maggie Simpson, Elizabeth Taylor, had entered her chambers.

More of her Merry Men followed, filling in the space behind her—a backdrop of complex shapes. She was a collector of rare specimens of humanity, a dream team from Central Casting. Jim Brooks stepped over to her, all smiles and admiration, and escorted her directly to her microphone at her stand. Her court, unsure of themselves in this foreign environment, trailed along with her. It occurred to me that the entourage was a bit like the dust clouds around Pigpen, the "Peanuts" character, constantly nipping at her heels, filling the space. Once she landed, they backed off to the walls, becoming a mere impression of what they were, shuffling into a tight little group in the shadows. Liz stood there confidently, an island, suddenly alone in the sea of studio space.

I watched her accepting or, more accurately, ignoring the looks of awe and adoration. This grinning look, which I'm sure others could see on my face, was not coming from all quarters, mind you. Some glares carried a very obvious challenge, as if looking for a chink in the chintz, a small flaw in the sea of public persona through which to thrust a dagger of wit. But, by and large, we were warming our feet in a pool of icon.

I couldn't help but imagine her as a bright, brash preteen with Mickey Rooney in National Velvet, all perk and positiveness, holding her horse's head gently in her arms and giving it the same love she now bestowed on her fluffy, white puffball with the pink tongue. Or working through scenes with Sir Richard in Who's Afraid of Virginia Woolf?, perhaps admonishing him: "Dick, this is a rehearsal, godammit! And could you please lay off the booze for five fucking minutes!"

She is all that a star—a galaxy—is, really. I couldn't help but wonder, Where can Liz go and not be known, seen in all her glory? I wonder if she is a big supporter of the space program in hopes of one day standing on a Martian desert, nothing around her but sand and silence. Even there, some spacesuited figure would probably hold out a notepad and pen, and with overwhelming admiration kindly request, "An autograph for my Aunt Sophie?"

The table we read around, a giant strip formed by several

long folding tables, complete with three odd-looking bulbous orange table lamps, has enough chairs around it to serve a royal feast. Normally, we would have our faces in our scripts, our heads facing the mikes that stood at the ready. But Liz had arrived and all the chairs, nay, necks were craned to get a full shot at this show. Elizabeth-fucking-Taylor was here and doing a voice on The Simpsons! How cool is that?! Today, we had a front-row seat to the best show in town, and I'm not talking about The Simpsons! Jim said a few words of welcome and then took his place with the rest of us, so Liz could do "her thing."

She was loving it. Her script lay there at the ready, the one line she was to vocalize highlighted to make it easy for her to see.

Sam Simon got the ball rolling, clearing his throat before speaking.

"Elizabeth, will you give us a sound check?"

The room fell silent.

She too cleared her throat and so did her dog, letting out a little whimpering sound. As we chuckled she gave him a pat of reassurance, faced the mike and out came the first words of Maggie Simpson:

"**** you, Daddy."

Of course Broadcast Standards and Practices, the division that handles what can and cannot be said on television, might have a thing or two to say about Liz's ad-lib. But then again, knowing Elizabeth, she might just say, "Off with their heads!"

NOTE: What eventually made the final cut was what was actually written in the script: "Daddy."

"The Fury Before the Sound"

Okay, okay, okay, you asked for it—and now I'm going to give it to
you. I know you are just dying to go "behind the scenes,"
to see Bart in his naked beauty, to see Homer in his girdle. By
now you may be thinking, "We're gonna get the real deal, the
actual making of the show. How they do it!" You want the
straight poop, the tool box, the plumber's crack, the shine on the
exec's shoes, the writer's bad teeth, the orchestra's passion? Well,
not only am I going to show you the puppet and the strings, I am
also going to toss in the stuffing and the stuffer. *I am Geppetto!*

Okay . . .

I have recently been very active on the college circuit, giving
lectures to the best and the brightest, who are on the brink of
making decisions regarding their careers, important decisions

about business, family and keggers. I love doing these show-and-tells. I always get a show of hands for: "Who didn't know that the voice of Bart was actually a woman?" I am always stunned to find out that there are still a smattering of people who don't know this, people coming to a lecture by Nancy Cartwright, the voice of Bart Simpson. "Whoa, is that who she is?" Well, maybe the best, but not the brightest. I suppose this book will dispel any rumors to the contrary . . . hopefully. Or, maybe not. If people want to believe in Santa Claus, let 'em. Some of the FAQs (frequently asked questions) that are popped back to me in the Q and A section are: What goes first, the voices or the animation? How long does it take to do an episode? Why do the characters only have four fingers? ("They can only count to eight.") Do you ever ad-lib? It's all done on a computer, right? How much longer are you going to be on the air? Does Matt do all the writing? I heard that you get a million an episode—is that true? and, Do you ever talk like Bart when you are having sex? (No kidding, this has actually been asked—twice!)

This chapter is dedicated to answering some of these questions. Okay, so how do we do what we do?

Oh, wait a second, before we get started . . . Even though I mentioned it in the introduction, the following is a disclaimer approved by my cats: ALL THE INFORMATION THAT YOU READ, ESPECIALLY IN THIS CHAPTER, IS BASED ON MY OPINION ONLY. I AM NOT RESPONSIBLE FOR ANY WRONG INFORMATION, MISLEADING INFORMATION OR ANY INFORMATION THAT I JUST DECIDED TO MAKE

UP. I DIDN'T DO IT. NOBODY SAW ME DO IT. YOU CAN'T PROVE ANYTHING!

Now, with the disclaimer out of the way, meoooooow, I just want to set the record straight by saying that extensive research has gone into the making of this book and *especially* this chapter. I've *tried*, people! Out of necessity, and out of just plain curiosity, I have immersed myself in the actual production process. Voice-overs have always been my passion and I finally got bit by the bug to explore more in the development arena. My own animation production company, Happy House, is a direct result of this curiosity and expansion. It's the house that Bart built.

The process starts with a pitch. A writer will present his idea to the rest of the team. How long it takes them to *get* an idea ready before they present it and where these ideas come from is a great mystery. Harlan Ellison, famous sci-fi writer whom most of you probably don't know, likes to respond facetiously that he gets his ideas from Schenectady, as if there is some great repository of clever thoughts somewhere in the East. There is probably some long-lost clay tablet buried somewhere that lays down the Ten Commandments of finding an idea. It happens in the bathtub. It happens in the Vatican. It takes a moment and is perfect. It gets slaved over for ten years and never quite works, or better yet, it does.

In the early years, the writers did a "pitch fest" at one of the local, very upscale hotels, like the St. James Hotel in Hollywood or the Loew's Hotel in Santa Monica. The whole day was contrived to get Jim Brooks out of his office and *off the phone*! They would meet for about eight hours. All the writers came totally prepared, with all their brilliant ideas stuffed in their heads. They would pitch two or three ideas for each episode and then Jim would just run with it. Mike Reiss, one of the original writers, said that "Jim writes comedy the way Mozart wrote concertos." Picture the hotel room, classy without being overly so, and nine grown men sitting around with their eyes and ears firmly glued to Jim Brooks, who is the center of attention.

"Okay, the basic idea is that Marge takes an art class . . . and she paints disturbing paintings." And that is all he would say. Jim then would start pouring out all these ideas, like coughing up a fur ball of comedy—he couldn't contain himself.

At the end of the day, they would have half the season's shows outlined. Of course, some of these ideas never turned into shows. They weren't all glorious gems waiting to be mined, but for the most part, they accomplished more in one day than most shows would in six months.

Oh, to be a fly on the wall! Most of these guys were single, young and broke. They absolutely had a ball. Food was brought in. Empty trays were taken out. Let's not imagine what these guys ate. Fad diets for writers probably consist of healthy doses of thick crust pizza, Jim Beam and ranch dressing. Several breaks were scheduled so the team of writers could stretch their legs as well as air out the room. I can only imagine that when you are coming up with new story lines for twenty-two episodes at a shot what the b.o. accumulation might be. (And I don't mean "box office!") Acceptance of an idea by the group divided by effort to make them love it equals level of body odor. Those ideas are so good, that room must smell like . . . P.U.!

One of the proudest moments of the writing team of the fourth season was with the show "Krusty Gets Kancelled." Mike Reiss, who was in charge at the time, had the idea to do a show with as many celebrities as possible—"and pack 'em in one big episode!" The problem was that the guest stars kept canceling! No sooner had they booked one, when another would fall out. It just didn't look like it was going to work. They almost had to pull the plug on the whole deal, but Bette Midler saved the day! Pretty soon everyone else was coming on board. This was right after Johnny Carson had done his farewell on *The Tonight Show* and Bette, being a real mensch, was willing to do a reprise of her farewell to Johnny on our show. To her credit, this was the one show that Johnny ended up doing *after* his retirement. Mike was pretty overwhelmed in the booth, during the recording session. It is the one taping that I wish I had never missed. This was another "Swartzwelder classic." And to add to the honor, *TV Guide* recently named it one of the top 100 episodes of television—ever!!!

OVER the years, "the team" has changed dramatically. To date, we have had five sets of writers, all under the supervision of one of the executive producers, otherwise known as the show runner. The title alone conjures up images of some "super jock," sprinting by in a pair of track shoes and a headband. He has a stopwatch in one hand and precious scripts clutched in the other, episode to episode, season to season, "Show Runner-Man." He is the guy who gets some of the credit when the show is fantastic and *all* of it when there are problems. Sam Simon, Mike Reiss and Al Jean, David Mirkin, Bill Oakley and Josh Weinstein, and Mike Scully have all been in this challenging position. I have no doubt that this is one of the most stressful jobs. That's why they get "executive" in front of "producer," as their Fox title.

It has been fascinating to see the show change and grow, and these guys had a lot to do with it. The tone, the stories, the style of the various seasons pretty much rise and fall on the influence of the show runner. According to David Silverman, one of the lead animation directors, "Sam Simon was very committed to the humor. He would reassure the writers that if the joke was funny the first time that it would remain funny after hearing/seeing it twenty times!"

I remember the first time there was a turnover in the writing pool and Mike Reiss and Al Jean stepped up to bat as the first duo running the show. There was genuine concern as to whether or not this was going to work. You get used to the bear having one head, not two. They were quieter in their approach, more subtle, if you will. But it was clear to me that their collective style was very different from what we had been doing. Better? Perhaps, but that is more a matter of taste. Different? Most certainly, but Matt's concept has always been elastic and new blood has always been able to pump through the show's veins.

David Mirkin brought in a new perspective. He was the only show runner to come from outside the "family," not being a part of *The Simpsons* until he came on board as the show runner. This posed an interesting challenge—to understand the show and maintain its success, while putting his personal touch on it. The fine shows during his reign speak for themselves.

Josh Weinstein and Bill Oakley were part of Mirkin's writing team and gradually moved into the show runner slot. Their style was more along the "Mike 'n' Al" line, but they added their own flavor, kicking the show into yet another echelon of popularity. Notably, they took the more psychotic Homer and toned him down a bit, making him more of a lovable idiot.

Currently (or at least as I am writing this book) Mike Scully is sitting in the hot seat. He has held the post for four seasons, twice as long as anyone else. Although he comes from a background of stand-up comedy and television writing, what makes Mike really stand out is his casual, "I'm-the-dad-let's-have-pizza-and-sno-cones" attitude. The fact that he and his wife, Julie, also a writer on the show, are the proud parents of five daughters might have something to do with that! With *The Simpsons*, Mike was adopting an eight-year-old kid, so to speak, and had all the challenges that go with new fatherhood. And in addition, this baby was inheriting a whole new set of uncles and aunts as we hired new, younger writers. I swear, some of these guys weren't even born when we first aired! The fact that Mike could keep the show going, and has been instrumental in a whole new *Simpsons* resurgence, says something pretty spectacular about him. I guess the whole "family" concept just suits him well.

These behind-the-scenes heroes are responsible for: seeing that the script itself is in top form; overseeing the animation director and making sure that he or she has the same vision in mind for the look of the show; working with the actors to get however many takes are needed to get the best performance for editing purposes; staying in close communication with the composer, who totally handles the musical score so it beautifully enhances that show; and making sure the continuity (how the show flows from one moment to the next) is consistent. In general, the show runner is the chief guy in charge of the complete and total look, sound and feel of the show—the foreman on the factory floor saying, "Let's get to work!" or the stage manager calling out, "Places!" He, as all show runners have been men so far, can be your big brother, the one everyone relies on. He earns every cent. Amen.

I would imagine that one of the most frequently asked questions for a show runner would be, "How long does it take to do each episode?" In a nutshell, from inception to air date, about eight to ten months, depending on how complicated the animation is and how intense the musical score. If you figure a couple or three months for writing and development and six or seven months for the actual recording, mixing, animating, editing, rewriting and on and on . . . yep, eight to ten months. Although that may seem like an extraordinarily long period of time, keep in mind that come the middle of the season, six or seven shows are being developed simultaneously. If we were to concentrate on only one show at a time, we could air only one show every nine or ten months! Get the picture of how much production must be going on in order to complete a whole season of twenty-two episodes? It blows the mind! Show runners never sleep. And neither do writers or animators. I personally believe they survive on Starbucks and nachos. Regardless, they are crankin' out a staggering amount of work. Believe me, when that two-week vacation comes but once a year, I wouldn't doubt if they spend the entire time sawing *zzzzzzz*'s.

Typically, an episode of another animated show will get pitched, written and then rewritten before it goes into the animation phase. With *The Simpsons*, however, once the show has been pitched and approved, it goes back and forth among the writer (one guy) and the rest of the writing team (eight to twelve people, with some of them not actively involved but available as "consultants") approximately *eight* times. In the process, ideas are suggested and changes made, honing, sharpening and clarifying the piece.

The writers who have worked on *The Simpsons* are the best in the business. They are an eccentric bunch, as varied as any group of workers could be who have gone out looking and ended up finding the greatest job in the world. (The late great producer Irving Thalberg once said, "The writer is the most important individual in Hollywood. And never let him find out.") I must admit that writers have a certain shared characteristic: They are incredibly quiet. Of course there are always the exceptions. Conan O'Brien was anything but quiet. Why do you think he got his own talk show! Apparently he acted out all the parts, from Bart to Burns, entertaining and cracking up all the other writers. On the opposite end of the spectrum is John Swartzwelder, who is still contributing scripts to the show in our twelfth season, although we haven't seen hide nor hair of the guy since 1992! To date, John has written fifty scripts, making him the most prolific writer of the show. He claims Carl Reiner is an idol for having written fifty-five *Dick Van Dyke Show* scripts. Surely, a new record is in the making.

The name you see on the credits under "Writer" goes to one person only, but in actuality, that writer is backed up by at least a dozen or more professionals who have, in one way or another, contributed to that script. Whoever gets the credit is the guy who actually physically sits down and writes the show. This has always been the way our writers have worked: It is about 70 percent original and 30 percent collaborative.

The pitch parties with Jim Brooks stopped several years ago. I'm sure that those were some of the best of times, being with such a master of comedy and, in the same breath, I have no doubt that the pressure must have been enormous. But then again, Jim has that laugh that is worth a million coins with Jebadiah Springfield's face right on them! Jim remains involved, but understandably at a distance. It is always good to see him at the annual premiere party or at some award show or presentation.

The annual excursions to some hot-spot hotel eventually became pitch meetings back on the lot. I can just imagine what it must be like to have spent months poring over a hot computer, slicing this, spicing that—all in the hopes that that script will make the cut. I wonder how a particular script gets selected. Is it done by lottery? Auction? "Hey-we-got-a-script-here-got-a-script-in-good-shape-opening-for . . ." Drawing straws? I can just see a roomful of writers all hawking their scripts to the show runner! "Mike! Over here! What?! His?! Why? You call that a story?! I'll tell you a *story!*" And what is there for the "bridesmaid" standing there after the decision is made, no bouquet in hand, watching the smug victor go off on a honeymoon to consummate a new creative union? "Who do you have to sleep with around here? Homer?"

In actuality, it is done quite sanely. Sometimes the room is full of other writers and sometimes it is a one-on-one with Mike. If there is one particular writer who is on a roll and ends up pitching several very good ideas, chances are that he will end up doing some of the stories, but not necessarily all. Because of the commitment to the script, one writer just can't handle too many.

The writers also have to keep in mind how many Bart stories there are and how many Homer stories there are, not to mention Lisa, Marge and countless other characters on the show. The idea is to keep a balance with all the characters and never let one dominate. Homer's intelligence level (or lack thereof) tends to put a lot of emphasis on Homer plots, since the humor factor is so high. This is yet another challenge for the writers. Also, they can't have the family travel from France to Australia to Capital City every episode either; with Homer's income, it wouldn't make economic sense!

When I asked co-executive producer Ron Hague how they continue to come up with story ideas after having done over 250 episodes, he says, "There absolutely aren't any more ideas . . ." But then he goes on to say, ". . . but we always manage to do it! Life is rich and there is still plenty to drain from."

ONCE the script is in agreed-upon good shape, it is ready for the official table-read. This is arguably the most exciting aspect of the process for all concerned, short of seeing it for the first time on television.

After having recently returned from the U.S. Comedy Arts Festival in Aspen, Colorado, I personally have no doubt that yes indeedy, the table-read is the most exciting aspect of the show. The fact that it is *live* makes all the difference in the world. It is just that the show itself is not a live-action medium. But there is no denying, when you sit in that conference room and hear the actors inject life into the black-on-white, you can't help but thoroughly enjoy yourself.

After months and months of writing and rewriting, this is the first time out of the chute. We get to hear it and so do the writers. This is crucial because, for the first time, the writers get to get it out of their heads.

The actors are delivered scripts late Wednesday night. In fact, mine is still left in my mailbox way past midnight and I don't even see it until the morning of the read. First thing I do is find out from the Cast List what characters I will be playing in that episode. Then I go through the script and mark all my lines with a highlighter. I used to actually mark all my separate characters with a different color highlighter: fluorescent yellow, orange, blue, green. This was just to make doubly sure that I wouldn't get any of my characters confused. 'Round about the middle of the second season that stopped. I guess I was a little more organized than I needed to be. (A skill that has served me more than it has harmed me.) Then I go back and start to read it. I look up any words I don't know—I am a dictionary freak! Every time I see Professor

Frink in the episode, I know I am going to be referring to my Funk and Wagnalls. What is a "glaven" anyway?

I remember the first season. Because I came from a voice-over background, I brought along the knowledge I had accumulated over the years. I remember telling one of the production assistants at the time to have a supply of highlighters handy for us. He hustled out to fulfill his new task.

The other actors have their own ways of preparing. Dan, Hank and Harry get their scripts delivered with their lines already marked. That totally makes sense—they usually have the most lines in any given show. Yeardley, Tress, Pamela, Karl and I highlight our lines ahead of time. And Julie, the most daring, doesn't mark her lines at all and has yet to miss one in a record! How do you do that, Jules? This is for both the table-read and the record. I prefer to "do it myself" because it gets me a little more connected with the script . . . literally.

Once I have my lines marked, I am off to Trailer 746 where we have been doing the table-reads for the past ten years. The trailer is located near the back end of the lot, across from Steven Bochco's "palace" and near the soundstages where they shoot *NYPD Blue* and *The X-Files*. We use this lovely trailer because, well, er, because that's where we go. It has a conference room that seats about thirty around a table and another sixty around the periphery. We can cram in another ten or so by slightly bending the fire marshal's limits. The "audience" mostly consists of production staff: writers, their assistants, production assistants, talent, publicity and assorted friends/family of all of the above. Occasionally we will get a winner of some obscure contest and his or her family. (Guess why Bart only has four fingers and win a visit to the Fox lot!) The contest winners and family/friends are the most interesting to observe because they have this fixed gaze of curiosity. This is usually a first for them: the first time hearing a *live* reading of the show, the first time seeing the actors voicing the characters, the first time they have ever been to Hollywood. Pretty fun. The room itself is barely large enough for the conference table and chairs. Another table is wedged up against the wall, laden with assorted bagels, fruits, coffee and juice. Nothing glamorous for decor at all unless you think a couple of posters from *The X-Files, Dharma and Greg, King of the Hill* and *The Simpsons* are glamorous. Hey, whattaya want?! This trailer could have ended up in Kansas, housing a family of six with three mutts— appearing one day on a news flash as it floats down a river in a flood. Instead, it's home to a bunch of L.A. nuts making a social satire. Go figure.

The table-read begins at ten although we don't usually get started 'til ten after—traffic and doughnuts. Typically, Dan will sit to my left and Yeardley a seat or two to my right, although in the latter years she has been gravitating more toward the end of the table, which is fine because if Bart and Lisa are in a dialogue together . . . "The better to see your face, my dear." We all float a bit, depending on who is sitting down already. Julie usually sits by Harry who is next to Matt and directly across from me. Hank, who has been working on one film after another and hasn't been around a whole heck of a lot, usually sits wherever . . . no bigga deal. Pamela, Karl, Marcia and Tress are scattered all around, making it one "bigga family."

For the last couple of seasons, there has usually been one or more of us who will be on location in another state working on another production. Recently, both Dan and Julie were in New York working on separate plays. During their absence, a speaker was centered in the middle of the conference table with Julie and Dan on the other end of the line. It was pretty weird, and definitely funny, to hear their voices coming out of this little black box.

It used to be that we would just show up and start the read, but as the years progressed, more and more requests would come in for the actors to autograph posters and scripts. These come from various nonprofit organizations, fund-raisers, schools, fans and friends of actors, writers, etc. We all do it, some with more pleasure than others. You can guess where I am on this. "This is great! Is that Allen with an *e* or an *a*? And he's how old?" These signed scripts, 8 × 10s, and posters have garnered lots of money for these organizations, but more importantly they have made some kid (even those over twenty-one) very happy.

A production assistant—a.k.a. PA—is an overall gopher of sorts—"go-fer this, go-fer that." This is the support position at the base of the production totem pole, and they work their butts off! No doubt about it, they get a cardio workout, running around doing this and that. The jobs that they complete, from making copies to running errands related to the show to getting signatures to setting up and cleaning up a room for production are extremely helpful.

A big part of a PA's job is making sure that all is well in hand and then making for darn sure that it stays in hand. Granted, the orders, from "Run off five more copies of this" to "Make sure it's decaf," may not seem very enticing to those considering taking on a PA's job; but I have yet to meet one on the show who just wanted to be a PA. Some of the perks include getting a well-rounded knowledge of how this show operates and learning who's who in the animation industry and being savvy to behind-the-scenes gossip. Though they don't get some of the perks that someone else higher up the production ladder might get—like an occasional box of merchandise or luggage with the Fox logo imprinted on it—they tolerate all the abuse because most of these young folks have dreams of writing and producing. Getting their foot in the door by being a PA can be a valuable start.

One young guy, Joe Boucher, started out as a PA on *The Tracey Ullman Show* and was brought over to *The Simpsons* by Gracie Films producer Richard Sakai. Because of his good work and attitude, he was hired and immediately promoted to post-production coordinator, who makes sure that all the postproduction activities, including recording of the voices, editing and transfer, are done. Joe was eventually promoted to postproduction supervisor, heading up all the postproduction from Gracie. From there, he moved on to associate producer, coproducer and finally, producer-producer!

When Joe first started on *The Simpsons*, he admitted, "No one knew what they were doing." They were all learning as they went along and, in fact, since no one had any preconceived ideas, "not knowing" was a good thing. When he was first hired he did so many different jobs just to "get the job done" that now it takes ten people to do what three people did in the beginning years. Joe, and producers Larina Adamson and Mike Mandel, helped to establish the "nuts and bolts" of postproduction that continue to be the modus operandi today. They created standard procedures for use in the recording sessions and the written forms to go with them; they worked out the correct method for ADR in coordinating the actors' and writers' schedules; and they established a way to keep track of the recording so the editor would be able to do his job expediently. Gracie gave them the opportunity to figure this all out and grow accordingly. This untried system worked so well that other prime-time shows have incorporated it for their own use—that is one indication of just how much *The Simpsons* has carved the way that others benefit from. Currently Joe is working on *King of the Hill* as a producer. When I asked him what the funnest part of his job was, without hesitating he said, "Seeing the cast! It is like watching a radio show and experiencing it." His dream is to nurture the artist in himself and to continue writing his own projects. This is one success story from a "lowly PA."

I would imagine that the best part about being a PA on *The Simpsons* is going back to a high school or family reunion or just out with your friends. Poised at the dartboard in the local pub: "Yeah, I work with Bart. She's cool." "She?!!!" Ah, to be an insider.

AT about 9:45, a PA will set a portable tape recorder on the table in the area where the actors are seated. This is strictly for the writers to use later as a reference. Sometimes the actors will ad-lib and this will ensure that the exact wording will be duplicated later in the rewrite, *if* they use it.

Dan, the king of ad-libs, has the most marvelous, unassuming way about him. He is extremely humble in such a charming way, very "un-Homerlike." His intelligence and clear-headedness are, paradoxically, one of the factors that allow Homer to come off as foolish and ridiculous as he does. He shines at the table read. He has set the table on a roar too many times to count. He will get so caught up in doing Homer that he adds a whole new dimension, adding a little "Homerism" to a line. "Mmmm . . . doughnuts," is the perfect example. There's no "Mmmmm" on the page. We die. "Mmmmmm, window washing fluid." "Mmmmm, root canal." Deservedly, Dan has received *two* Emmys. In the ad-lib department, Hank's Professor Frink could almost say anything and be guaranteed a laugh. You can imagine how much self-control it takes in the recording booth, where they also ad-lib mercilessly. And if Homer and Frink have a dialogue—egads!—you might as well stuff a sock in your mouth!

I personally find that ad-libbing is very dependent on what character is saying the line. I don't ad-lib a whole lot for Bart. I find that when I stick to the script, as written, I deliver the best Bart there is. Ralph Wiggum, on the other hand, can practically say anything. "My cat's breath smells like catfood" gets a laugh every time I say it. "It tastes like burning!" and "I bent my wookie!" are guaranteed gut-busters. Why? I think it has to do with *who* Ralph is. He is such an innocent kid—the fact that he just glued his head to his shoulder is very funny because poor Ralph just isn't quite all there.

We read through the entire script with one of the producer/
writers reading in all the descriptions, locations and directions.
FYI, our staff writers aren't just writers. They have also been given
a producer moniker in some shape or form—executive producer,
co-exec producer, producer, co-producer, consulting producer and
consultant to name a few—depending on how long they've been
on the show and where their strengths lie. So they become writer-
producer, consultant-writer or whatever. What's in a name? No
one really cares. At least I don't. They join the select group of
talent in the industry better known as "hyphenates." They pull in
a paycheck for writing and get the prestige of a "producer" on
their resume. The "Produced by" credit on screen that America
sees will eventually go to a line-producer, someone in a producer
position but involved administratively as opposed to creatively. (If
all this sounds complex, relax, no one in Hollywood really un-
derstands it either.)

Ideally, the entire cast is present for the read. If, for some
reason, an actor is missing, either they are piped-in electronically—
through the phone and speaker system—or someone else is kindly
asked to read their lines in lieu of. It is not a good thing to miss
the table-read from the writers' point of view. This is their shot at
hearing the dialogue and visualizing the story from beginning to
end so they can do their rewrites. If one of the actors is missing,
it truly makes a difference in the read. The other actors fill in and
make do, but to have someone else read my part must make for
a strange-sounding Bart. After all these years, the sound is so imprinted in our minds that to hear another do it sounds inappro-
priate. And you don't get those ad-libs! I apologize in advance if

I am asked to do Lisa when Yeardley is missing. Hey, better me than Harry, Hank or Dan!

When I have missed a table-read because of another job or because I was in labor (true story) it's like missing out on a really cool field trip. It is such a delight to go to these readings—they throw me back to high school when I competed in Reader's Theater. Truly a rare art form now, due, no doubt, to the invention of television. (Sniff.)

Once the table-read is over, we all give ourselves a big hand and go our separate ways. The applause has been the tradition with the show since the very first read. Considering the battery of work that has gone into the show up to this point—the idea, the pitch, the writing, the printing, the collating, the delivery, the set-up, the questions, the scheduling and because it is Los Angeles, the *traffic*—it is the completely justified acknowledgment! But this is just the toddler's first step, as you are about to find out.

The writers go back to one of the larger rooms in the writers' building right there on the Fox lot and talk over what they just heard. They make comments and suggestions about what stays and what goes and come to an agreement on those changes.

The writers use their own personal rating system to determine the value of the humor. If it really busts a gut, it might get *****. If it gets a pretty good chortle, it might get ***. And if it only gets a little snicker, it wouldn't get much more than *. Of course, if the thing really bombs, I would imagine their scripts would be filled with lots of *!!?%$?!!*??!?!* So, whether they use *** or !!!! or $$ (hee-hee), each writer has his own method of indicating the laugh-factor for that particular joke or image. During the table read, it is a pretty funny sight to see all twelve writers mark their scripts simultaneously. Of course, when they get back to the conference room to go over what they just heard, I can just imagine some of the discussions. I am sure they don't always agree on what worked and what didn't.

"What about this moment here when that smell cannot be located?"

"I thought it was funny."

"It only got one *."

"I gave it !!!"

"Come on, it wasn't even worth half a *."

"Yeah. I don't think repugnant body odors go over very well, no matter whose body they are coming from."

"I have to agree with you, Jeb. Body odors are gross and disgusting."

Okay, maybe they don't quite go that way, but you can be assured that they thoroughly go over every single, solitary, potentially funny, if only a tee-hee laugh and then decide whether to keep it, change it or dump it altogether. According to Mike Reiss, "There is no ego. There isn't any time for that. Most of our attention is on 'Does the story work without it?' And who is gonna get laid tonight."

"It's Not Unusual..."

We have a tradition at chez Cartwright. The tradition goes back for nigh on twenty-one years, although I wasn't always a part of it. Good friends of ours actually had this tradition but they eventually invited so many people that they ran out of space. They needed a bigger venue, *and* we love them, *and* we love parties, *and* because we live on what used to be a farm . . . (Take a big breath, here!) there is plenty of room to have 250 of my closest, most personal, best pals come to celebrate the anniversary of our independence. (Whew! I am exhausted and need a nap.) Every Fourth of July we have a huge blast. ("Blast?" Sorry about that, but there is no other way to describe it.)

We have been hosting it long enough now that it is a tightly choreographed celebration. Behind the scenes of all the family fun, there is a military network of seamless perfection. It is a potluck, so everyone with last names from A to F brings salad; G to K brings veggie dishes; and so on. Long tables stretch end-to-end on our tennis court. No games in progress, please! They are patriotically decorated with all the red, white and blue bunting you can muster and salute. Sterno at the ready. We rent porta-potties and hand-fashion direction signs, so you can go from here to there and there to here without getting lost in the environs. In addition, the signs serve another function: They keep the partiers outside where they belong! We have Ping-Pong, swimming, water balloon fights and "Rest Areas" for those that need a break from all the high-cholesterol food. I recently incorporated a new item to make communicating to the chosen few easier and less stressful on my vocal cords. (They *are* insured for a million dollars, after all.) And yes, I admit that this purchase was more for my own personal pleasure than for health reasons, but who can resist an air horn from Radio Shack? We use one occasionally on the show and I thought, What a cool toy! I simply must have one. So when a new guest and his or her family arrive, I introduce them to the crowd. "Ladies and gentlemen, Carmella and Michael have arrived! Let's give them a big hand!" And they do. Then, for the poor soul who forgot this was a potluck, "Ladies and gentlemen, Clem is here and he didn't bring anything! Go sit in your car!" That only happened once. He has a nice car.

We take great pride in the entertainment aspects of the event. In fact, over the years it has developed into such a production that we are getting requests from bands to perform. Izzy's Old Enough to Know Better is our blues headliner, which might have to do with the fact that it is Izzy and his wife, Mary Ann, who are the other hosts of the party! Actually, his band is so hot, they would get the gig even if we auditioned all week. But prior to introducing Izzy, we rock out to our jukebox of one hundred CDs of the best of the best music ever. I just program it to play a random selection and it goes on and on for hours; and I don't just play any cut from any CD, mind you. I am very selective about which ones make the grade.

It has become a tradition of the tradition to kick-off the party with my most favorite CD of all time and that is *Tom Jones' Greatest Hits*. It rocks. Pure and simple, it gets things goin'. We have speakers all over the place and kick up the volume to about 10½ and party down. (We always invite our neighbors, by the way. We find that is the best way to stay neighbors.) I just love this CD. It has a rhythm and a pulse that is electrifying. In fact, I program the jukebox so that every fifth CD is this one. It will guarantee one of several outcomes: You will learn all the words to all Tom's hits and possibly choose skintight spandex as your fashion signature, or you won't come back next year, or you'll just feel it and who knows what will happen when you get your sweetie home that night? Let the party begin! The CD silently finds its "groove." And Tom's rough, dulcet voice works its magic on the toe-tapping revelers celebrating our nation's birth. It is a sound that has come to have a deeper meaning for me. I sip an iced tea and remember the day I discovered the power of Tom Jones . . .

WHAT *a total blast from the past! No, a blast from the now! I just got home from a musical scoring session with Tom Jones! Omygod! I am in love! He is so incredible. What a talent. What a bod. What a set of pipes! I have never been to a scoring session before but had been given an open invitation; and I thought, Tom Jones? Okay, yeah, all right. All right??!! (Down girl, down!)*

The session started at 7 P.M. at the end of a long, long day. It was my weekly night out and I had ducked out before family dinner time, not an easy feat with a baby and a toddler. I nestled into my pink Miata and headed down to the recording studio, leaving all household responsibilities behind, not really wanting to. Jack had me up most of the night last night, strange dreams roaming through his sweet little mind. Lucy is cutting some new teeth. It's pathetic when 7 P.M. is "late," but a mom always has an excuse. I hope I wasn't a road hazard, but I'm not sure I was all there.

I had picked up a CD of the man, of Tom, earlier in the day. I was a sing-along fan, nothing too crazed, but I always liked his sound. Now, I was listening to some of his standards, "What's New Pussycat?" and "Delilah," trying to get in the groove. I found my fingers drumming, my body swaying a bit but I couldn't quite get in the mood. My cell phone was right there. I could call and make my excuses, go back home and curl up with the kids and hubby for storytime, my favorite time of day . . . But I kept on cruising, the music moving me forward through the evening traffic.

When I arrived at the studio they were already in full-swing, so to speak. I stepped into the booth that looked down on the vast, open recording space. I stood there for a moment, the glass separating me from the action. Tom was behind the mike and Alf Clausen, The Simpsons' *conductor-extraordinaire*, was on a little platform with baton in hand. Alf records with an orchestra—no synth for him. The musicians were out there, arranged in neat little rows, about thirty veterans of studio work, artists who we have probably been hearing for years, anonymous geniuses who give us joy and in return ask only that we listen.

There was a huge screen to the left showing the animation for the episode. They were into a real upbeat rendition of "It's Not Unusual." Alf, his arms flying, conducted Tom and the musicians, keeping them in time with the flashing images of Springfield. The song starts during the very last scene of the show ("Marge Gets a Job" by Josh Weinstein and Bill Oakley). Tom has been kidnapped and is shackled to a stage by Mr. Burns. So, here I am, watching Tom Jones do a parody of himself . . . live. He's loving it. I'm loving it. The song is supposed to continue over the credits so Alf and Tom just carried on. Omygod! Tom Jones rocks! They put on a full-blown production! The band went wild. The song going on and on. I danced and danced. At one point Tom looked up and waved to me and I waved back, never missing a beat. Finally, Alf brought them to a close and I gave them a cheer they couldn't hear. Alf must have seen me leaping like a crazed grasshopper because he glanced back and gave me a wave. "That's Nancy, everyone. The voice of Bart." The guys waved. Tom bowed. Then they went back to work, Alf giving them notes, *a tempo here, a timing adjustment there. I leaned back into the soft couch and smiled, oozing into the cushion, the music still moving through me. Tom had just become my fantasy come true!*

I had already met him earlier at the initial dialogue recording session, back in April. He was gorgeous. We really hit it off. "I love Bart," he said. He loves me, I thought. I remembered every detail of that first visit. His scent. He invited me to come see him. You have to go, I thought. He invited you and a guest to the MGM Grand in Las Vegas . . .

And there we were, me and my sweetie. It's like a dream . . .

The leggy-miss, sporting a Vegas-tan-in-a-bottle, escorts us down the aisle of the glitzy auditorium. We end up smack-dab front-row-center orchestra. We glide our dressed-to-the-nines selves to the best seats in the house. Excellentness. Tom arrives. It's a religious experience—the religion of hips. His voice, his passion gets him panting and swaying, the music thumping. There is this sound that forms a background. I can't quite make it out. Suddenly, it occurs to me: It's the sound of women swooning. How completely silly, I think. But I feel it. It comes through the floor, vibrating up into my feet and my gluteus minimus, and within moments, the sensation takes over. Power, oh, baby, power. I can't help myself! I'm into it. It's the pulse, the beat, the rhythm, the hips, the pelvis, the passion—I find myself having this incredible urge to merge!

Next thing I know, Tom is reaching down and grabbing a hold of my hand and is pulling me up onto the stage with him! Omygod! He is singing "It's Not Unusual" and I just can't seem to stop "merging"! We are movin' and groovin' to the music and he is swinging this and rotating that and everyone in the audience is screaming and loving it! I become the expert dancer I am not. I am "in-sync" with all the gyrations of the universe, the planets, the moons and stars, all things that inspire poetry and cuddling. He is twirling me and dipping me and practically flipping me but I don't mind! Hell, no! He hits the song's climax by lifting me up in his arms, spinning me around and around and around, the crowd dancing into sight and back out, his smile glistening in unison with the giant sequin curtain, the glow off the band's instruments. The swoon in the crowd turns to a cheer. He sets me down. I can't breathe, don't want to breathe, I'm all breath, a breath as big as the stage. He is beside me, flowing love at the crowd.

"Thank you. Thank you," he says. "You know what a thrill it is to be here." They cheer. Why am I still here? I wonder. He goes on. "I've been performing at the MGM for about thirty-five years now, and have done over 4,000 performances worldwide." His arm comforts me, allowing me to stay, giving me courage to look into all those beaming faces. "I recently returned from a concert in Amsterdam and when I got off the plane I was nearly mobbed when the entire crowd was chanting, 'Simpsons! Simpsons! Simpsons!' The episode that I was on had just appeared and it was all the rage!" Now, we are all applauding and a low chant starts up way in the back. "Simpsons, Simpsons . . ." "My 'dance partner' is a special guest." I feel the blood leave my feet and take the freeway to my scalp. "You wouldn't recognize her but I am going to blow her cover . . . Ladies and gentlemen, the voice of Bart Simpson, Nancy Cartwright." The spotlight hits me like a shot. Instantly, the crowd surges to their collective feet. They

applaud, they laugh and chant, "Bart! Bart! Bart!" The lights twirl all around and suddenly balloons, streamers and confetti begin falling all over the place. Bells and whistles struggle for supremacy. "Bart! Bart! Bart!" I enjoy the moment. The band picks up . . . "It's not unusual to be loved by anyone. It's not unusual . . ."

"Nancy?"

I look up but Tom isn't speaking to me.

"Nancy?"

The sound, the cheers fade away, receding, going out of focus.

"Wake up, kid, we gotta go."

I opened my eyes and found myself still in Alf's studio. Alf stood over me where I had sprawled out on the couch. Tom was down on the soundstage, shaking hands with the musicians.

"You want to say so long to Tom?"

I smiled. "Yeah. Yeah. I do."

"Well, come on, Delilah. He's waiting."

And I did. . . . Hey, a girl can dream, can't she?

"The Sound After the Fury"

Come Monday mornings, the 405—the freeway for us valley people—or the PCH—the highway for those Malibu people—traffic permitting, we gather once again. This time we meet to tackle the actual recording of the show. It used to be, for the first few seasons, that the first order of business was an additional table-read wedged in before we would get to the mikes. This would be followed by about a half-hour break for us voices, while the writers would convene and work notes, make changes. This frantic scribbling used to continue throughout the day. As we were recording, we would receive different color-flashed pages, to replace the scenes that had been given a final touch-up. The first script (table-read) was always on white paper, then it went to blue for the record. Throughout the day as we laid down the voice track, we would receive yellow, green and, when those writers' imaginations were extremely overactive, pink pages. As the new pages came in we simply exchanged the old for the new. The actors knew that the writers were burning up the ink when the pink ones showed up!

We abandoned the second table-read about three seasons ago. There were mixed feelings regarding this. Everyone got out of there faster, no complaints, while at the same time it eliminated another go-round of new ideas, scenes, etc., that had contributed to the overall understanding and concept of that show. I miss the additional read. I think it helped the actors review the flow and rhythm of the show and the writers got to have another chance to brainstorm. After the Thursday read-through, we don't see hide nor hair of the writers again and while I simply miss seeing them enjoy the fruits of their labor, I also worry about these guys. Writers with free time . . . not a pretty picture. Nowadays, if we don't get it right, the watch word is "We'll get it in post." Ah, the responsibilities and mysteries of postproduction, a world we will glance into later.

We do the initial recording on the Marge Simpson ADR stage, which was recently built in honor of the mom who helped to build Fox Broadcasting into what it is today. Way to go, Marge! All our mikes are lined up next to one another in a circle, à la old-time radio. (Picture George Burns, Gracie Allen, Jack Benny, Bob and Ray, June Foray, Mel Blanc and Daws Butler.) One of the writer/producers who will direct the actors is seated at a table. Occasionally Mike will direct us, but his duties as show runner generally demand his attention elsewhere. I'm sure he'd rather be with us—working with "the stars behind the stars." It adds a nice diversion to the day. Louise Jaffe, our script supervisor, sits to the director's left. Her job is to keep track of who is reading whom and the number of takes being recorded so the editor can paste it all together. She also has the demanding job of keeping us kids in line when we get to gabbing about some current event or gossip. I guess Marge isn't the only mom in the room! Occasionally, the writer of the episode is there too. I am sure that he/she must have feelings similar to an expectant father's or perhaps even a mother in labor. Some of the newer writers are so interesting to watch at the record. They wear an expression of reserved fascination. They tend to mind their own business. A lot of the young writers we have were just out of high school when the show first aired. And here they are, working fans, like bat boys who made it to the team. When they first start I think they are a bit in awe of the whole thing. I can only think of one time in all the years that a writer asked for my autograph. And when he did, he had me sign everything from clocks to posters to scripts to dolls. Go dude! I think he mentioned that he had twenty-two nieces and nephews all under the age of twelve! No wonder. I wouldn't mind signing for these artists till I got writer's cramp. *The Simpsons'* writers walk where few have tread and I see them as the backbone of the show. They are the font from which all this brilliancy has originated and if in signing a Bart clock or calling one of their relatives on the phone I could somehow show how much I admire their work, then it would truly be my pleasure!

As we record, the writer sits huddled off to one side with the director. Most of the actors will do the first take as written. It will at least give the writer a chance to hear his masterpiece. I will even do it as written for the second take. But come take number three, I will add a word, a thought, a comment, if I feel it enhances the dialogue. And I will do that again for another pass. If we do a take five, I will tend to go back to the written script. I have never noticed a writer get upset because I've changed something. They seem pretty open-minded in that area. But if they aren't quite getting what is needed from the record, they will consult with the director and changes are made. "Nancy, can you do it again . . . and just read what is written this time." Okay, so some of my ad-libs *don't* end up on T-shirts! Can't blame a girl for trying!

Like a standard sitcom, the script is broken down into acts and scenes. Unlike most standard sitcoms, we don't rehearse, we don't do a camera-block, there is no live audience and we don't have dressing rooms. Actually, the first season we did have trailers. Union rules. They lasted about three hours. We were all in just about every scene so they were virtually useless. "I'll be in my trailer! I'm resting my vocal cords!"

It's rare that the actors don't contribute something to nearly every scene in the show. There are plenty of crowd mania scenes with packs of kids, doctors, lawyers, agents, professors, mobs, medical students, advertisers and assorted animals that we are needed for. We once recorded a doozy that required lots of animals. We went around the room, actor to actor, groaning, snorking and honking assorted creature noises. It really doesn't get any better than this.

OUR schedule has gotten so pat that we don't even take time for lunch any longer. It truly is an embarrassingly effortless job at this point. We work about four hours straight and that's it for the actors on that episode. Months later, whether we are recording new shows or on hiatus, we are brought back to record any post-production "clean up" on that show. All in all, it adds up to about six hours a week. (I'll pause while you pick your jaw up off the floor.)

Okay . . . I am sure that you are saying to yourself, "Six hours a week! You have got to be kidding me! What a piece o' cake job!" No, I'm not, and yes, it is. To be on one of the highest-rated, highest-acclaimed and arguably the funniest show on television and only have to go to work six hours a week sounds like a crime! Guilty as charged.

Yes, and most actors can't wait to have a jail cell of their own. No doubt about it, there has been a huge increase in the number of thespians who would give up a shot at Broadway for a chance to voice an aardvark in Disney's next classic. Thing is, they don't have to. You don't have to give up your night job. Six hours a week? Sick. Frankly, the explosion in production of other animated shows and films is a direct result of *The Simpsons*. Twelve years ago doing a voice-over job was a novelty but now, because of the lure of "easy money," it's become something of an obsession. (And thank you, *Daily Variety*, for publishing my weekly salary for all the world to see.) I can't count the number of demo tapes actors have asked me to review. I just about always say no, or quality time with my family would consist of baritone car ads and falsetto parrots. "Kids, we have a special demo tape tonight for your bedtime story!" "Not again, Mommy!" The starving actor is lured by the dream of some easy cash and a chance to have some fun at the mike. He sees himself as the next Homer or she sees herself as the next Bart. But it's not just the pavement-pounders who want the smell of the mike. Numerous celebs step up for the kick of it or for bragging rights—"I was Bart's lover, who the hell are you?" And then there is that strange breed, like myself, who actually set out to do this from the start. It wasn't about money or the cushiness of the gig. It was about years of classes, studying tapes, working on characters, developing new ones and enduring many auditions and rejections. Being any kind of actor is not an easy task, but when it comes right down to it, the cash one gets doing an animated character, at least a regular one, for the amount of time spent is, well, enviable.

To give you an idea of how different the voice-over world is from the on-camera world, my good friend, Leah Remini, who stars in *The King of Queens* on CBS, has clued me in on what it takes for her to do one episode of her hit sitcom:

"I get a new script on Friday. On Monday morning at ten there is a table-read. While the writing team and producers go over notes, I discuss the costumes for the show and then we start the initial blocking. I am out of there by four o'clock. A new script is messengered to me that night.

"Tuesday and Wednesday it is more blocking and run-throughs, more rewrites and then we reblock with the new script.

"Thursday is blocking for the camera all day. It is tedious, arduous and very technical. I drag my poor dogs home around seven.

"Friday is makeup/hair at eleven. We continue with camera blocking and tweaking all day. At six-thirty sharp, we are introduced to the live audience and then we start the show. We'll do each scene three times. We are usually finished by ten.

"We are constantly changing lines, adding jokes, fixing jokes, cutting this and shifting that. We do this schedule for three weeks, then take a break (hiatus) on the fourth. By then, I really need it."

I feel *so* guilty! Plus don't forget all the paparazzi, the rag-mags, the invasions of privacy, especially when you're out on a "date" (even with your spouse!). And one of the biggest barriers for that on-camera star to overcome: typecasting. This is the downside that goes with the job and is part of the reason that on-camera talent get such big bucks. It is all relative.

ONCE the voice track is recorded, the show runner and the editor go through all the selected takes and decide which one to keep as the final choice. Just imagine what that must be like: listening again and again to the same line, over and over, trying to figure out which one is the best one. Over the years, this process has been streamlined in the production phase by having whoever is in charge of the record make notes in the script as the actor adjusts his take on the line. The slightest changes are indicated, as it makes the editing process go much faster.

Occasionally one of us will volunteer another take because we feel that somehow a better read is in there. And most of the time, we are right. We are all pretty good at that. The willingness to do the reads again and again, to make sure that we are all satisfied, is a big part of the reason why the show remains consistently good. But when it comes right down to it, I would never know one way or the other. The actors don't have any say as to what take will be selected. And truth is, it doesn't matter anyway. By the time the show airs, so much time has passed that I don't even remember the plot, much less the "right" take!

This completed sound track is then sent over to Film Roman in North Hollywood. Of all the odd jobs a PA has on this show, I don't think one of them is delivering the sound track to the animation studio. I heard a rumor that Fox actually kicks in the cost of an armored truck to deliver this precious cargo. You can hear the *007* sound track playing under the narration of Troy McClure. "It was a tough job. Dangerous? To some maybe. To me? Just part of the job."

Film Roman, the animation company that does all the preliminary artwork for *The Simpsons*, is a well-oiled machine. They animate *The Simpsons*, and have done so for years, as well as animating *King of the Hill*. Recently, I took my staff, family and friends there to get the nickel tour. They were all given the royal treatment, while I was escorted to a special room to sign various animation books, posters and even the arm of one truly dedicated fan. To let the staff know that I was there, I got on the P.A. system and in Bart's voice said, "This is Bart Simpson. I am in the employee lounge for all interested parties. If you want to get my John Hancock, bring all materials and a check for $50!" Of course, that last bit was a joke, so I laughed as Bart. Needless to say, I never did get the nickel tour. It was later, after I started this book, that I realized that I should probably back up my opinions with some factual data. And thus, several more tours and lunches took place, wining and dining the powers that be, with tape recorder in hand, while I culled the information regarding the actual animation process. Apologies in advance for leaving anyone out. And "wine and dine" is just a figure of speech—you didn't miss out!

So, I leave you for now to wonder at the mysteries of the world of animation, a world of pencils and fluorescent lights, cubicles peopled with artists hunched over new Homers, fresh Marges, Lisas and Barts. Their hands lovingly stroke to life an image of Smithers as he gazes with longing at Mr. Burns.

"And Bingo Was His Name-o"

► MAY 21, 1993

I *am sitting here in my office. It has a distant view of Glendale's Forest* Lawn *Cemetery and overlooks the 2 Freeway. Our view gets you going and coming. One of our dogs, McGuffy, a feisty little "Heinz 57 breed," is by the door. He is the official family sentry. One ear is constantly at attention, even if he is not. Hey, you never know what marauders you might find in Glendale.*

I just laid baby Jack down for his nap and in my hands is a letter that I received today from Ernest Borgnine. Before I gathered the courage to open it, I suspected that it would be a "chill out" letter because I had been such an over-the-top nut fan when he had walked in the door to the recording studio recently to tape an episode of the show. Finally, I took a deep breath and I broke the seal.

The stationery is very simple, with "Tovern Productions" at the top. His wife's name is Tova. He is Ernie. Tovern Productions. Get it? It's a family thing. In the letter, Ernest lovingly remarks about how his granddaughter, Shelby Lynn, is fighting him for the Simpsons' jacket he was given after the record. I relaxed as I read, there being no mention at all about my initial freak assault. It is amazing how one little thank-you letter confirmed so much what I had seen in him that day. But then again, in his case, I am not surprised at all. With Ernest Borgnine, what you see is what you get.

I hadn't known this or really much at all about him except that he was McHale and in the navy. And I could never forget how his Oscar-winning performance in the 1955 film Marty changed me forever. I had seen the film years before—before Bart was a twinkle in Matt's eye—before I had discovered that I wanted to be an actress, heart and soul. This was the performance that made me realize that actors have the power through their work to inspire and enlighten others.

Paddy Chayefsky had written this stunning piece with tons of golden nuggets for the actors to mine, and Ernest Borgnine broke my heart and anyone else's who saw him in this film. I empathized with Marty, "an ugly man," not that I ever considered myself ugly, but I just never thought my physical appearance was my calling card. What really got to me in this film was the universal truth about who someone really is. You are not your body. Or, it's what's inside that counts. Or, you can't judge a book by the cover. Take your pick. This theme has been explored a billion times but not quite in the sensitive way director Delbert Mann did *in this film. There is this one line when Marty is talking to Claire, his love-interest, and says, "I'm the guy they gotta dig up a date for." Again, it's not that I am cryin' in my beer here. I'm not. But the pitfalls of dating and homecoming and the prom were very real for me. I dated a little, but thank God for Sadie Hawkins dances. Without the "turn-about" I don't know that I would have had any dates! I filled the time happily enough, pursuing my own personal dreams and goals—even on a Saturday night! I spent my spare time in the marching band or on the speech team going to tournaments. I did gymnastics and community theater. I was pretty focused on doing the things I loved. But there was some major loneliness when I would see other young couples doing what young couples do. My sister, Mary Beth, would help me get through the tough times when I would wonder why I didn't have a boyfriend or even a date. She reminded me, as Marty did, that I was beautiful.*

Marty was so gorgeous within. More people can relate to someone like that, at least physically, than to, say, Clark Gable, Paul Newman, Tom Selleck or Matt Damon. Marty is the male precursor of some of the great female characters like Georgy Girl or the Shelley Winters character (who loses Montgomery Clift to Elizabeth Taylor) in A Place in the Sun. Marty sets the stage for Rocky Balboa and his plain-Jane girlfriend, Adrian. These characters are the crème-de-la-crème. They are the parts that Oscars are made for and the parts I ultimately saw myself playing.

Years later, I found my Marty. I became smitten with Giulietta Masina's portrayal of Gelsomina in Fellini's La Strada. Then came my aforementioned trip to Italy to find

Fellini to get the rights to do a stage version of the film. Now, that was a Sadie Hawkins moment.

At the table-read for "Boy-Scoutz 'N the Hood," it was noted in the script that Mr. Borgnine was going to be joining us later in the week for the record. I thought, That's cool. No problem. I didn't know that just below the surface lurked Super Fan! On record day, in he walked—and I totally lost all coolness! Suddenly seeing him in person—it was like I was really seeing Marty! My throat got tight and dry. My hands started to sweat. The little hairs on my neck started to tickle and suddenly I am rushing over to him, gushing, "Omygod, Marty!" How embarrassing. It's a wonder they didn't call security and have me escorted off the lot.

I have a treasure trove of keepsakes that includes the auto-graphed 8 × 10 I got from Red Skelton (when I was ten) and the letter inviting me to Italy I received from Fellini's office in Rome. I will place Ernie's note among them. It reads: "Can't tell you when I have enjoyed doing a show more . . . because I have never done it before. My thanks to you all, for being so kind and helpful. I don't think I will ever forget B-I-N-G-O, . . . but I'll try! Really, it was a ball!"

He apologizes in writing, as he had done on the soundstage, for not being able to sing. The camp counselor he voiced had to lead the kids in a rousing chorus of "B-I-N-G-O." It wasn't that bad! I had a roommate once who was tone deaf and had this habit of singing lustily every time she vacuumed. And McGuffy some-times sings to the moon and the stars, thus inciting all the dogs in the neighborhood into a 2 A.M. canine sing-along. Ernie wasn't anywhere near that bad. No, he does himself an injustice. I had heard his glorious "sound" once before while visiting a friend on the maternity ward of St. Joseph's Hospital. As I stepped in, a celestial chorus of wailing babies sang to me from the nursery. Now that *is a much more accurate description of Ernie's pipes! It was—how do I say?—inspired by a higher source!* Or, perhaps his source is an eternally youthful one, the voice of a child. Like I said before, with Ernie, what you see is what you get. Or in this case, what you hear.

No one minded what key he was in at all. I personally think it added to the authenticity of his character. After all, how many camp counselors are opera singers, or even musical comedy performers? (Hey, if Marlon Brando can do Guys and Dolls, *then* Ernest Borgnine can play a singing camp counselor!) The show turned out fine.

As we wrapped up the day, Bonnie came back in the room to escort Mr. B. to his car. She presented him with the much-sought-after Simpsons' jacket. They are really cool—like a varsity football jacket, with red leather sleeves and plenty of room for our "letters," or in this case, embroidered patches of our characters. It really is quite an impressive fashion statement. And for a second there, watching him slip the jacket on, I caught another little glimpse of that sweet character that Ernest had created all those many years ago. He smiled his Marty smile. "Thanks!" he said. And broke my heart one more time. Bingo.

My Mom Is Bart Simpson

I love being the voice of Bart. Make no bones about it. I don't think I could have dreamed up a better gig. It is almost as if "destiny" had a name for me and that name was Bart Simpson. I share this passion with . . . myself, not that the other cast members don't have a passion for their work on the show. I believe they do too, but the degree of that passion varies from one to another. I also believe that there is a lot of responsibility in upholding the reputation of the character who *Time* magazine considers to be one of the top 100 entertainers and artists of the Twentieth Century.

I wear Bart on my sleeve, so to speak—or actually, I carry him around in my hip pocket, ready to whip him out at any given moment. I have been asked to do and have done literally hundreds of interviews over the last ten years. I'm quite a "yes girl" in this area, an "easy chick" you might say and I wouldn't slap you. I know that once an interview is over, I have the security blanket of anonymity on my side. I just go back to being Nancy or wife or mom or writer or producer or artist or whatever. This may all sound rather self-serving if not somewhat narcissistic, but believe it or not, self-love is not what fuels my engine. (Excuse me for a moment, my pedicurist has to shift feet. Ahhhhh . . .)

At one time Yeardley used to drive a white Miata. I loved her car. It was so cute, almost like a toy. In fact, I liked it so much, I had to have one. And I figured that if I was going to drive a toy car, it had to be pink. There was just something about the size and shape of that car that demanded pinkness. I don't mean Pepto-Bismol pink and I don't mean the Mary Kay Cadillac pink. I mean pure and undeniably *bubble-gum pink!* I had so much fun driving that thing! Zipping here, zapping there and all the while making people do double-takes on the freeway. I was the personification of pinkness. In fact, someone said to me once, "Your life is a pink Miata!" I believe the comment was well-intended to get me to self-reflect on my overly ebullient nature, but . . . I couldn't have been more pleased. The problem is: Some people just can't stand that color!

One afternoon, I was zipping along—love the sound of that motor!—when a flashing red light caught my eye. I quickly pulled over onto a side street and shut down the engine. Busted. As he eased his overly muscled physique from his black-and-white I ran down the list of potential excuses: Late, nah; pregnant, not this time; overactive bladder? Uh . . . nah. (I have since learned from my friend Camryn Manheim—thanks for the tip, honey—that what you have to do is cry. "There was a car following me!" Or "Did you see that squirrel I ran over?" Something to elicit sympathy. She once succeeded in getting a police escort!) He ambled up, already filling out his ticket pad, and arriving at my window he grunted, "License and registration." He didn't even respond to my blond smile as I handed him the papers. I found myself saying, "They say red cars get pulled over more than any other color." He just stared and, of course, I had to explain! "Uh, mine's kind of, well, pink, not exactly red." Then a weak laugh. He glanced at me, clearly thinking I was a pathetic wanna-be in the smooth-talk department. Then he headed back to check out my plate.

As if the lurid pink paint job wasn't enough to turn heads, and some stomachs, I had one of those annoyingly personal license plates: DNTHVCW. Who could ever figure that out? I was used to some pretty funny looks. Unfortunately, this cop was no different.

He walked behind my car. I turned and watched the whole thing. He stood there and looked at my license plate and literally scratched his head with his pencil! He came over to me and said, "Your personal license plate could cause an accident, you know . . . people trying to figure it out and all." It was clear he didn't know what it said. So, in Bart's voice, I snickered, "Well, don't have a cow, man!" Lead balloon! He was more than annoyed now. "What is that supposed to mean?"

"That's what my license plate says—DNTHVCW—Don't have a cow."

He just stared. I fumbled forward like a sheep going over a cliff. "Have, uh, have you ever watched *The Simpsons*?"

"No."

Strike two.

"Oh, well it is a very popular show and I, uh, I do the voice of the kid who says, 'Don't have a cow, man.' "

He cocked an eyebrow. Uh-oh. "Listen, lady . . . I don't care who you are. I just stopped Nicolas Cage in his brand-new Ferrari and gave him a ticket. You were speeding and now you are going to pay."

Strike three. Lesson learned. Case closed. And I *tried* to lighten up on my foot from then on. Note the operative word, "tried." I just loved the sound of that motor!

THE novelty of the car eventually wore off and I got sort of tired of being the center of attention every time I got into the cute thing. I ended up donating it to a fund-raiser auction for Narconon, a very successful drug-rehab program. I suggested they ask blue-book, $7,500. Turned out that Olympic athlete and heavyweight champ George Foreman was receiving a Drug-Free Hero Award and he ended up buying my car. He announced for all to hear, "Miss Cartwright, I am going to donate this money to the Narconon because I believe in this program, but I am going to give you back your car because I ain't gonna be drivin' no pink Miata around Los Angeles!" I was exuberant! I couldn't believe it! Here I was, back in love with my car again. Not five minutes later I was practically knocked over by an enthusiastic friend. "Nancy!

Nancy! I can't believe it! All I wanted was to buy your pink Miata! And I got here late and I heard that George Foreman just bought it and now I am sad—what am I going to do?" My pink bubble just burst. I looked at her and, with far less enthusiasm than she was feeling, I said, "Just give Narconon $7,500 and let me drive it once in a while and it's yours." Well, that's exactly what happened. Carina drove away in her new car, Narconon got a $15,000 donation and I got to baby-sit it every time I needed to goose the Miata in me!

JOURNALISTS tend to love these stories, especially if he/she is the first to hear of it. It's colorful, pink even! But "first" only happens once so the trick to a successful interview is to make it sound like the first time, every time. Being a stickler for records, I was able to review some of the interviews I have granted. I have articles and some transcripts as well as audio and video clips. There were some winners and some losers, both on my part and on the part of the interviewer. Where do some of these scribes come from? The questioners were at times grossly uninformed: "So, you're the voice of Lisa, right?" And at other times out-and-out mean: "When did you drop your lawsuit against Fox?" What lawsuit? I thought about culling the best and worst but instead I created an interviewer, Mike Raphone, to get "up front and personal." The first thing I notice is that Mike needs some exercise and probably smokes, but he would never let on. Digging deeper, since he's my creation, I find that his friends think he's smart but they don't really like him much. Okay, he doesn't really have any friends. He has associates and they don't like him either. But he can turn a phrase and his uncle is a top exec with *Time* magazine, so his job is secure. Let's join the interview, already in progress:

Mike: I think the question that most of your readers want answered is whether your children know you do the voice of Bart.

Nancy: (I'm wondering: Did he actually poll his readers to get that question?) Of course they do.

Mike: Really? I would have thought you wouldn't want them to grow up with that type of role model.

Nancy: Well, first of all, they know the difference between a cartoon and reality. And Bart's not such a bad role model.

Mike: Excuse me?

Nancy: No, that's fine. Here's a hanky. You don't watch the show much, do you?

Mike: Well ...

Nancy: He's actually very sweet, loving at times, with a sense of humor.

Mike: I see, well, then ...

Nancy: They're actually proud of me. Or at least as proud as they can be at their ages.

Mike: What do you mean?

Nancy: Well, since I am the only mom they've known and I have played Bart since before they were born, they take it in stride. I don't try to get my kids to promote for me, but they tell their friends sometimes.

Mike: And their friends expect them to act like Bart?

Nancy: No, no. They never, well, rarely, act like Bart.

They didn't really get the public significance, between me and Bart, until they were eight or nine years old. I knew that my little guys fully understood the brownie points Bart could bring when I was recently performing at a church charity benefit for underprivileged kids. At intermission I went to check on them in the audience. I saw my son and I came up behind him. He was sitting in front of the stage surrounded by a sea of blue Cub Scout uniforms. These kids were from the ages of five to eight . . . adorable. When I tapped him on the shoulder, he turned to me and squealed, "Mommy!" Suddenly I found myself drowning in a sea of excited boys. "Do Bart! Do Bart!" And I did and they just loved it. It took a bit of doing to get the agreement of seventeen Cub Scouts to sit and watch the rest of the show. I promised them that I would be back afterward to talk and sign autographs. This seemed to do the trick so I started to squeeze through the blue maze, heading backstage. I had to turn to take one more look at that undulating blue sea. Just then, my son stood up and announced to the whole troupe, "See, I told you my mom was Bart Simpson!"

Mike: But the kids at their school don't know about it!

Nancy: Are you kidding?! I am the most popular mom there!

Mike: And is that a good thing or a bad thing?

Nancy: Oh, no one takes that seriously. Their knowing is a good thing. It keeps everyone quite entertained. And the other students know my name—

Mike: Bart.

Nancy: Nancy, they call me Nancy. I don't hear them calling the other parents by their first names. I think this is because early on when they found out I was Bart's voice, they all started calling me Bart. I didn't like that and didn't feel it was right. After all, I am not at work and I am a mom. But at the same time, they are young fans and love Bart and really light up when I do the voice. So when they say, "Do Bart" I give them a little with an appropriate "No way, man!" and everyone is happy.

Mike: When was the first time your kids realized that you were Bart?

Nancy: My son was two years old. I remember standing on our back patio, holding a talking Bart doll. This was a prototype to see if the public was interested in buying talking merchandise. Anyway, the doll had one of those pull-strings in his back, but it was a little short, so it sort of sounded like he was on helium. (Pull string.) "Don't have a cow, man!" (Pull.) "Eat my shorts." (Pull.) "I didn't do it!" That sort of thing. Well, my son was pulling this string and listening, very entertained, when he turns to me and says, "I don't see you in there, Mommy. I don't see you in there."

Mike: Pretty high concept for a two-year-old!

Nancy: Yeah. But Lucy realized when she was nine months old.

Mike: Nine months!?

Nancy: Sort of. We were recording "Lisa's Substitute" back in 1990 and Sam Simon asked me to do the whimpering for baby Maggie. She never speaks, at least not until years later when Liz Taylor provided her immortal voice saying "Daddy." I've done plenty of babies and was about to lay it down when in walked hubby Murph with our little Lucy in his arms. Omygod! Lucy . . . Maggie? What do you think, Sam? Always a gamer, Sam gave the go-ahead. I held Lucy in my arms right in front of the mike. I whispered, "Roll tape." It was perfectly quiet and I moved to hand her back to Murph and she let out three little whimpers . . . perfect, real, one-take. What a pro!

Mike: But it's not like she really knew!

Nancy: Maybe not, but they grew up knowing, hearing Bart in the womb, so it seems natural to them. I will have parents come up to me, when they find out I am Bart's voice, and demand, "Do Bart! Do Bart for little Johnny here." And their poor little kid, usually two to four years old, will be standing there with a total look of confusion on his face. This little guy has no clue about the process of voice-overs and I find it upsetting that a parent would insist I "do Bart" when the truth is, it is more for him (the parent) than for his kid. When this first happened, I went ahead and did the voice, but the reaction from the kid was not at all good. It was just what I had suspected all along. Nine times out of ten, the child will get upset, hide in his mommy's skirt or bury his head on his dad's shoulder. I felt responsible. So, once I saw the effect I decided that I would never do that again. I have to get the interest and curiosity from the kid, not the parent. If a parent does that to me (requests that I "do Bart,") I will tell them no. It just isn't right.

Mike: You'll snub a fan, then?

Nancy: Ab-olutely! [sic]

Mike: Really? And when you are making love to your husband, do you ever use the voice of Bart?

Nancy: Bart? No, but Marge's voice turns him on a little. What about you, you think Bart is sexy?

Mike: Uh, well, he's only ten. That's a little odd.

Nancy: Agreed.

Mike: Point taken. Let's see . . . tell me other instances when you refused to do Bart.

Nancy: Well, as you're recording this, right now—

Mike: Oh, of course, I wasn't suggesting—

Nancy: That's fine. I have to make it crystal clear when I do a recorded interview, especially for broadcast. The fact that interviewers will be told, even sign something, and *still ask* for some free Bart surprises me every time. The prohibition has to do with legalities, copyright infringement. It is a funny thing but although I own my voice, I don't own Bart's voice. It would stand to reason then that I couldn't just go out and in Bart's voice say, "Even though you think I am Bart Simpson, I am actually Nancy Cartwright and you're listening to KBBL." These legalities are common in television/film production. The actors don't *own* the characters they are doing. They are owned by the creator and/or the studio/production company. But I don't know that Jennifer Aniston is being asked to "Do Rachel!" or that Brandy is being told, "Do Moesha!" With on-camera actors they can drop a line in, a parody of themselves, but it's different in voice-overs.

So, just as we did today, we'll make a deal. No new Bart lines. But nine times out of ten, they will sheepishly ask, "Hey, before you go, could you just say, 'Hey, this is Bart Simpson and you're listening to Newt Sidenbender in the Morning!' " Absolutely ridiculous. But don't get me wrong, I have no problem whatsoever "doing a little Bart" for the listening audience. I can do whatever Bart would typically say. All those expressions we have heard a million times and have seen on all the T-shirts, candy jars, backpacks, ties, etc. And I can say funny lines from the scripts because they are documented expressions. The trouble comes when I am asked to originate a line. This is *verboten*.

Mike: Well, I certainly won't break that rule today.

Nancy: That's good or I'm outta here, man!

Mike: Touché. Have you ever used the voice to get something you wouldn't normally have gotten, say as just a normal television-watching public?

Nancy: Could you be a little more specific?

Mike: Have you ever used the fact that you are Bart for your own . . . gratification?

Nancy: Look, here's the deal. I use Bart, but I never feel I take advantage of people. For example, I recently went over to Melbourne to make a guest appearance at the Comic Art Gallery. Just prior to catching my plane, I caught a cold. By the time we were airborne, I also had laryngitis—not a good thing for a voice-over artist! I was absolutely parched and kept bugging the flight attendants to get me more and more water. I began to feel too demanding because I wanted so much more than the glasses they were serving. Finally, I wandered back to the galley and struck up a conversation with the crew. The passengers were asleep, so I wasn't taking the crew from their jobs. I started, "Listen, I know that I am beginning to be a bit of a pest. Is there any way that I could just have one of those large bottled waters? Then I won't have to bug you every fifteen minutes or so."

The one gal looked at me and immediately slashed out, "Absolutely not! We don't have enough to go around. You'll just have to make do." Here we were on an international flight and they don't have enough water? You have got to be kidding me!

Rather than lashing back, almost always a bad strategy, I said, "Okay, fair enough. Can I have another glass then please."

As she grudgingly poured I put the wheels in motion. "How long have you been a flight attendant?"

"About seventeen years."

"Wow, that's incredible. I guess you must really like it."

"Yeah, it pays pretty good and I like the time off so I can be with my kids."

"How many do you have?"

"Three, but only one is still at home."

"How old is he?"

"He's fourteen."

"Fourteen, eh? Does he watch *The Simpsons?*"

"Oh, yeah, sure . . . everybody does."

And then in Bart's voice I said to her, "That's really cool, man." She was holding out the glass to me and she stopped dead in her tracks. "That was pretty good."

Knowing she was still not convinced, I went on, "Thanks, man."

Now she started to smile and shake her head in disbelief. "Are you the voice of Bart?"

Back to myself, "Yeah, my name is Nancy Cartwright."

"Omygod! He is gonna die when I tell him you were on this flight! He is such a fan. I have always wanted to do voice-overs. That is so funny. And here you are on this flight."

And we continued to have a very in-depth conversation about her and her dreams. I gave her some career tips for voice-overs. She told me what it takes to be a flight attendant, emergencies she has handled. So, you see, even though I really just needed some water, it didn't look like I was going to get it without using the "persuasion of Bart." It ended up being fun for both of us.

Mike: Yeah, but the big question is, did you get your water?

Nancy: Oh yeah, in fact when I sat down with the liter, next thing I know another flight attendant came up to me with another whole bottle!

Mike: Was there any time when it wasn't a good thing to be the voice of Bart?

Nancy: Uh . . . yes. There was this one time when I was at a track and field event watching my son run a bunch of relay races. I was sitting behind a group of parents who were having a discussion about television and how they don't like what they are seeing. And they started commenting on the various shows.

Mike: Did they mention *The Simpsons*?

Nancy: Yes. In fact, the one mother said that she would never let her kids watch it because she felt that it had a bad influence on them.

Mike: What did you do?

Nancy: I tapped her on the shoulder and I told her that I couldn't help but overhear and that I was the voice of Bart.

Mike: What did she say?

Nancy: Well, she was totally taken aback. I didn't mean to embarrass her, but if someone is going to make a statement like that, they should be responsible for the effect it could create. As a part of this show, I realize that Bart is not a good role model, mostly. But that doesn't mean the show is bad for you. People aren't influenced that easily anyway. It just means that whoever is complaining about it hasn't watched it all the way through. And I told her that. It certainly didn't win me any popularity points with her. I am sure she felt horrible. But that's what I do when school principals, religious zealots and parents who are narrow-minded take a stand on something that they haven't fully investigated. *It is satire, folks! Get it? Satire!* We are poking fun at life and people. Sometimes it seems that America is losing its sense of humor and *The Simpsons* serves as something of a counterforce to all that seriousness. And besides, I am a mom and my kids have yet to *use* the fact that because Bart does things and gets away with it they can do the same thing. I teach my children the difference between right and wrong. Maybe what I was really doing when I caught that woman off-guard was actually busting her for not really being a responsible parent.

Mike: Pretty harsh statement.

Nancy: Yeah, well . . . that's the way I see it. I think it is important as parents to follow a guide, have a set of rules that you live by in order to teach your children right from wrong. Of course, if Marge and Homer followed that precept, we wouldn't have a show!

Mike: Good point.

Nancy: But you still get the idea that deep down inside they [the Simpsons] really love each other. And that is one of the reasons why the show does so well. It reflects what most American families are really like. You really believe that this is the truth.

Mike: Have you ever met anyone who didn't believe you were Bart?

Nancy: Oh yes. When my daughter was just a little baby I remember taking her to the mall. We drove a Nissan wagon that we had painted bright yellow and put these cut-outs of Bart's head on each side window. The license plate was ELBARTO. I remember getting out of the van and going around back to get out all the baby gear I would need to go shopping. It was a bit awkward, so I was struggling a bit when this man was walking by. He didn't stop to help. He just smugly said, "Wow, you must really love Bart Simpson." And because of the situation, I couldn't help myself. I told him to eat my shorts, just like Bart; and he turned to me and smirked. "That's not Bart. I know the guy that does him." And I said, "Oh really? A *guy* does Bart's voice?" And he goes on, "Yeah, that's right. Yours is pretty good, but it's not Bart." In a case like that, I don't even bother. It wasn't worth my time.

Mike: So you actually decide whether or not you are going to use Bart when you meet strangers?

Nancy: Oh yeah. When I meet people I like to get a sense of who they are. I think of it as a game. A lot of times I will discover that someone who initially comes off as kind of cranky and even rude will actually end up being quite an interesting person—if you can just get them out of the funk they are in. For example, there was this one time when my parents and I had gone to the Rose Bowl parade. After the parade was over, we went to the area where all the floats are on display. It was an absolute madhouse. There were hundreds, probably thousands of people, all trying to find a parking place and then get in line and wait another two hours before being herded like sheep around the display area. I spotted an attended lot with a Full sign and pulled in. The attendant was waving his arms and saying, "We're full. We're full. There's no more room." Well, I dangled a mid-sized greenback from my fingers, just to get his interest and get personal. He came around to face me, glancing at the cash. "Sorry, lady, but—" I cut him off. "Hey, are you a *Simpsons* fan?" "What? Uh . . . sure." "You got any kids?" Again, he doesn't know where this is leading and says to me, "Yeah, three." Now he is really curious and he is getting the look of recognition. "What if I told you I was Bart Simpson?" Suddenly his face lit up like a ten-year-old's. "Omygod! My kids will never believe this!" I pulled out a few "Read, man" bookmarkers. They are the niftiest little things—so much better than signing a napkin or a business card. [More about these later.] Anyway, I got his kids' names and handed them over to the guy and the next thing you know, some car is pulling out, leaving a space just for us!

Mike: So you ended up being the hero for your mom and dad.

Nancy: Yeah, and that guy ended up being a hero for his kids. That's what I love most about "revealing" who I am. I love the effect it creates when I surprise people with the voice. Almost every single time, they walk away feeling a lot better than they did before I "pulled a Bart." And I love that.

Mike: So you clearly don't mind having people find out that you are Bart's voice.

Nancy: No, not really. I mean, how much damage can I do? I only do this on a one-to-one basis. I like the challenge of changing someone's life, if only for that moment, for the rest of the day. By revealing who I am to an individual, it gives them something to share with others. And I think that is important. The truth is, I think living on planet earth these days is pretty tough. I don't envy my children one little bit. The pressures that they have on them in society are far greater now than when I was a kid—drugs, sex, what clothes to wear (or not), what movies to see, what music to listen to, trends, etc. Yes, I had all of that when I was a teenager, but because of the extreme advancement of technology (the Internet, VCRs, cable and Tommy Hilfiger, etc.) the kids of today have an even greater demand put on them to keep up with the Tiffanys and Devons. So, if I can bring a little lightness into someone's life by sharing that I am the voice of Bart, I'm just gonna do it. And I'll do it in any way, shape or form that I see fit.

Mike: So, in a way, you get the best of both worlds, then, don't you? In regard to being a celebrity *and* having your anonymity.

Nancy: That I can go anywhere and do anything, alone or with my family, and not be gawked at or judged or invaded when I am just having dinner in a public place *and* be able to whip out Bart's voice whenever I want is the most ideal scene for an actor.

   [He pretends to turn his recorder off and I know it's coming. This is where the interviewers always bombard me with those juicy questions. The nasty ones almost always come out, like the boogie man emerging from under the bed.]

Mike: So, just a couple more questions. You mentioned drug rehab. Any personal significance there?

Nancy: I'm a person. Recreational drugs and people do not mix.

Mike: Right. And, uh, I know it's been a while since your last round, but, uh, how long do you expect contract negotiations to bog down?

Nancy: What negotiations?

Mike: The pay isn't bad, is it?

Nancy: That's nunna.

Mike: Nunna?

Nancy: Yeah, nunna . . . as in "Nunna your beeswax!"

Mike: Well, I guess that's about it, Nancy.

Nancy: Well, thank you, Mike.

[I can feel it not far off, like the smell of bad milk.]

Mike: Um . . . er . . . before we finish, er, do you think you could just say a few words as Bart, maybe . . . (He holds out a sheet of paper) something like this? (reading): "Hey, editor dude, Bart here. Mike rules, man. He's totally cowabunga and if you don't print this whole article you can eat my shorts!" I smile and shake my head. Even in your imagination, they ask. They always ask. I pick up his handheld recorder, smile and directly into the mike I say, "No way, man!"

Could I Have Your Autograph?

▶ APRIL 22, 1994

O h man, did I ever blow it! She was right there! I was working right
beside her! I had every chance in the world and I freakin'
blew it!

Last week we got our scripts and it was printed right there:
Jessica Lovejoy—Meryl Streep. Who'd a thunk it? How cool is
that?! Then, at the table-read the next day . . . she wasn't there
but we hoped that she would actually come to the full-cast record.
Two days later at the record—no dice; her schedule didn't allow
for it. I was totally bummed! We recorded the show but skipped
over the scenes between Bart and Jessica, which was most of the
script. "We'll pick those up later, Nance." Yeah, right, "pick up"
with me alone, talking to myself. I was certain that she was
going to have to record her lines in some far-off sound

booth that I would never see but would always imagine. This isn't unusual with guest stars; there have been dozens that Bart has spoken to that I have never met. Although you'll get a better performance out of an actor when he or she is actually talking to another actor in the room, duh, the fact that it is "just the voice" allows for tremendous freedom—heck, you can literally phone it in! Once that group record had been completed, with no sign of Meryl, for me to keep hoping that I would meet her was—well, I'm me, what can I say?

I have been a fan since I first saw her in Julia. I lived in Ohio in that era, a tyke of _____ years old. (Don't think I'm going to tell you how old I was so you can use the film's release date to calculate my age. I'm in my thirties, and I'll always be in my thirties!) And although we Daytonians were very slow in getting answering machines and David Bowie LPs, we did keep up on Who's Who? in the entertainment industry. She was all the buzz. She came out of nowhere and delivered this bravura performance. The next year she was Oscar-nominated for her work in The Deer Hunter. As a theatergoer I have always been totally enchanted by her—sitting there, popcorn forgotten, Cherry Coke diluting with melting ice. There is something so pure, so luminous about her. She makes you fall in love. And what do we do when we love a star? We get her autograph!

So, yesterday I get the word that we're finally going to record those Bart and Jessica scenes and . . . "Looks like Meryl's gonna be there, Nance." Omygod! Two-thirty, at the Village Recorder in West L.A. A field trip!! We don't typically record there. Maybe it had to do with security—protect Meryl from hungry autograph *hunters, like* moi. *The Village Recorder is just a stone's throw from Fox and is most noted for servicing some of the top musicians in the industry, like Billy Joel, Bruce Springsteen and Madonna. (That would be kinda fun . . . to run into Madonna—after all these years! "Hey, Madonna, remember me? We used to work out together! You, me and the Wrigley twins?")*

I walked in—totally cool on the outside, gooey mess on the inside—and was greeted by the engineer and one of the production assistants. I signed my contract and got all the busywork out of the way as others and others and others were showing up. Where did all these schmoes come from? She's mine, dammit!

We were prepped and ready, a little nervous excitement in the air, when in walked Meryl! I couldn't help but notice the contrast with another guest star of The Simpsons *just two years ago. (Hint: ET . . . and I don't mean the funny-lookin' alien!) No fanfare. No entourage. No ring the size of Nebraska. Meryl is so cool. She's just a real person. She had on a simple khaki dress and espadrilles, her hair was shoulder-length and curled, she wore absolutely* no makeup . . . *and she was stunning!*

Introductions were made in a cordial but somewhat solemn tone down the long, narrow room. I had somehow positioned myself at the "Siberia" end, Meryl far, far away but moving slowly toward me. "Hi Meryl, I'm Bonnie, the casting director." And they shook hands. "Let me intro you around," she continued. "This is David Mirkin. He'll be directing you."

"Hi. Nice to meet you." Handshake.

"This is So-and-so and this is Blah-di-blah." People were shakin' all over the place, nodding their heads in sup-

plication. Come on, I'm thinking to myself. Come on! All the moisture from my mouth seemed to have migrated south and I was practically wetting my pants with anticipation. I had already publicly humiliated myself with the Ernest Borgnine debacle. I didn't want to do something like that again, or worse, be standing in a puddle when she got to me. Just a handful of producers remained between us. She was so close I could smell her. What was that lovely, delicate scent?

"Oh, and this is Nancy Cartwright. She is the voice of Bart." Meryl took a gasp of air. Sounding every bit like a ten-year-old herself and wiggling her fingers in a hello fashion, she squeaked, "Hi!" It totally broke the ice. Everyone laughed and we were on our way.

As we headed over to the microphones Meryl touched me on the shoulder and said, "I'm a little nervous. Are there always this many people at a record?" Wow! The espadrille just slipped on the other foot. I began to wonder, Maybe she has never done a voice-over job before. I scanned the pack that was watching us chat—eat your hearts out—and turned back to her and said, "Well, I think there are a few people who would probably love to have your autograph, if you know what I mean." Omygod! I can't believe I said that! You big goofball! Then I tried to repair the damage. "You'll be just fine. Just do that thing that you always do, Meryl." Omygod! Did I just say what I think I said? "Just do what you always do?!" Omygod! You're blowing it! I wouldn't give me my autograph.

We took our places at the stands and I busied myself arranging my script. My mind crackled along with the papers. I began to wonder how she would work with me as an actress. Had she done her homework on the show? Or is she a regular fan, simply enjoying the show with her family? Or, does she watch the darned thing at all? Will she be selfish, generous and/or meticulous in her work at the mike? Will she fulfill her reputation of professionalism, a fountain of ideas, the actor's actor? I would never go through the motions and phone in a performance, and I couldn't imagine her phoning anything—unless it were a voice-over! She could let it go today, not work with her well-known thoroughness and no one would ever hear the difference when the show aired! What's in this for her? Why knock herself out? I convinced myself, in about seven seconds, that I wouldn't see the real Meryl in action.

Her stand was right beside mine. Technically, this is not a good thing. In voice-overs, if you are doing an intimate scene or any kind of scene for that matter, where the characters really need to connect, the stands should be placed face-to-face. I decided to take matters into my own hands, sweaty as they were, and I asked the engineer if he could rearrange the stands so we could face each other. He got on it right away. She looked up, a bit confused as he came over to move her stuff. I explained. "It doesn't work if we stand side-by-side. You'll have to turn your head and that will take you off-mike, so facing each other is just common sense." To that Meryl added, "Well, after all, Jessica has to be able to flirt with Bart and you can't flirt with a boy if you can't see him." Slipping into Bart, I said, "You watch yourself now. I'm a married woman." And with this, she totally cracked up!

She laughed with such ease and grace. I watched her,

that easy smile that goes right up to her expressive eyes. All these years I'd imagined myself in her shoes; what it must be like to be recognized as one of the most prestigious and well-respected actors of the twentieth century. I had imagined what it would be like to work with her—but I always pictured it being on-camera! What irony to be here, working with Meryl Streep! I am not just seeing her from afar at some entertainment industry awards luncheon.

As the stands were repositioned and we could meet eye-to-eye, I said to her, "This is such a treat. I love that you are Bart's girlfriend."

"Yeah, you and my kids," she said.

I read somewhere that she has four kids and her husband is a sculptor. She lives far away from Hollywoodland, on the "right" coast. She doesn't come across as a shmooze type of actress, staying out of the limelight and the slime light. The National Enquirer is not putting Meryl Streep's face on the cover. My admiration for her was shifting into just plain liking. I dig this chick.

The engineers were getting a sound check from Meryl. Listening to her so-familiar voice, my mind went off on a journey I hardly expected. I was wondering what it would be like if our roles were reversed today. Instead of her being a guest on our show, what would it be like if I were playing the part of her best friend in some film. I've done some on-camera work, but my stomach jumped at the mere thought of it! It just wasn't as comfortable as voice-overs. But . . . and it hit me! Acting should never be comfortable! This is what had separated Meryl from the boys. And this might be what had led me to this far more "comfortable" world of voice-overs. Perhaps I didn't want the discomfort, the depth of commitment that characterizes Meryl's life. All this roaring speculation, these colliding thoughts and comparisons, went on, hopefully invisibly, between my ears.

In order to still the earthquake within, I decided to make conversation. I asked her about her kids. "So your kids are fans of the show?"

"Are you kidding! They never miss it!" she said. "My oldest son is fourteen and he hasn't seen any of my movies. They aren't interested in them and besides, they really aren't for kids anyway. But when I told them that I was going to be on The Simpsons . . . Omygod, the pressure is on! I have to do a great job!"

My heart settled into a more normal rhythm. I could leave my deeper questions about personal commitment aside. Today she was in my world. She wasn't quite sure where to put what and how to set up this and that. It was a complete and total surprise. Meryl needed a friend. Things aren't always what they seem.

"Are you kidding me?" I said. "You are going to be fine."

And with that, we started the record.

The episode, "Bart's Girlfriend," has Bart paired up with Rev. Lovejoy's daughter, Jessica. Although Bart is bad to the bone, Jessica is even worse. She has evil powers that can make boys do whatever she wants.

For example, in a montage, Bart and Jessica are leaning underneath a No Loitering sign. They periodically look up at the sign and share satisfied nods. Then Bart and Jessica stand in front of a window of a weight-loss center, eating a gallon of ice cream, rubbing their tummies and smacking their lips tauntingly at the overweight exercising patrons. And finally, Jessica and

Bart are running around, toilet-papering a statue of Jebediah Springfield. They are whooping it up and laughing a lot.

BART:

You're incredible, Jessica. Your throws, your catches, your spirals, your loops . . . It's like the toilet paper is an extension of your body.

JESSICA:

(SHYLY) Thanks, Bart. It's good to finally find someone who really appreciates me.

I wasn't the only one who was wondering how Meryl would work, what we would get of the "real Streep." We did our typical five or six takes on the first scene, each time adjusting the reading a bit to give the producers an array of choices. But after the sixth shot, Meryl scrunched up her nose and looked at Mirkin and asked if she could do it one more time. Of course this was no problem, so we did it again. Then after the seventh take, she scrunched up her nose a bit and again to Dave she said, "I have another idea . . . could I . . . ?" Without missing a beat, we were rolling again. Well, after the eighth time through, she wanted to do it one more time!

"Meryl, you're making me look bad!" I said. She smiled, a little embarrassed. And I'm thinking, What could she possibly do that she hasn't already done before? And darn if she didn't pull off yet another totally different take! We were getting the whole enchilada!

It is this constant diligence, her willingness to do it just "one more time" that has made her what she is. We settled into some serious work and I wanted her to go on forever. One of the lessons I learned in studying acting with Milton Katselas at the Beverly Hills Playhouse is that "attitude is everything." He stressed how someone can have all the talent in the world, but if his or her attitude about work and people stinks, then the talent won't have a chance to even be demonstrated. It is very clear that in Meryl's case she has an abundance of both talent and good attitude.

We finished the script and said our thank-yous and nice-to-meet-yous and headed toward the door. My mind was going a mile a minute. It's now or never, Cartwright! I was searching for a segue, some easy way to go from being peers-joined-in-the-work, to becoming completely separate—the fan and the star. "Can I have your autograph?" didn't quite fill the order. I didn't want to embarrass myself, in front of her or the others. But it was my last chance, maybe forever. I placed my hand on the doorknob, Meryl right behind me, and I thought, Do it! Ask for it! You'll probably never see her again!

"Nancy?" she said over my shoulder.

I turned.

She couldn't quite meet my eyes. "Do you think maybe you could give me your autograph? It's for my kids. They would really love that!"

She held out her script and her pen. Now this was surreal! I think I must have totally blanked out there for a second because I "awoke" to find myself stuttering, "Uh . . . uh . . . sure! That would be fine." My mind returned, slightly, and I

hoped my mouth was closed but I can't say for sure. "I have just the thing," I managed.

I whipped open my purse and I pulled out a handful of the Simpsons bookmarks that are put out by the American Library Association. They have the whole Simpson family flopped around the couch reading appropriate stuff for their characters—Marge, a romance novel; Homer, a TV World mini-mag; Lisa, a stack of Dickens, Plato and Voltaire; and Bart is upside-down on the couch reading a Radioactive Man comic book. The bookmark states: "Read, man."

"Those are perfect!" she said, all atwitter, the adoring fan.

I dashed off a few. Hey, you never know when Meryl Streep is gonna ask for your autograph!

I'm Talkin' to You, Cowboy ... Draw!

If your life were a cartoon, and pardon me in advance if your life is a cartoon *already*, someone would be following you around with a huge ream of paper, drawing everything you do. If your life deserved high quality you would be sketched at about fifteen to twenty-four pictures per second and if you were a sitcom each "episode" from your daily existence would be approximately twenty-three minutes long. (Give or take a few commercials.)

Alongside this very fast sketcher-without-a-life would be a geeky-looking guy holding a tape recorder. This highly sensitive device would catch not just what you say but anything anyone else says (Are you scared yet?) plus it picks up every sound, normal or embarrassing, that can be heard around you.

Another artist would madly sketch all the backgrounds

as he follows you everywhere, yes, everywhere you can go in twenty-three minutes. But because these artists are on a budget, and would probably die of repetitive strain injury, there are limitations. So, they select what to draw. You would notice that quite frequently objects and people around you would "freeze" and just your head would be moving, or perhaps only the background moves as you drive down the road. And, of course, whenever anyone or anything else moved into your space, they would have to be drawn in too.

Twenty-three minutes of your life not interesting enough? Don't worry about it! A writer would take care of that. Imagine yourself under the sea or in outer space. You could be in the future or in the past. He could take what you have in life and make it funny. Your family and friends would all be very interesting. Yes, even that aunt of yours who smells weird. Your life would go places you never imagined.

Let's say you have a boring face. Don't worry about it! If you don't cut it as you are, he'll give you that extra something that makes the difference—maybe a bigger nose, dainty feet or delicate hands, four fingers instead of five, a wife with a strange hairdo. But, again, because of the budget, the color scheme would be a bit limited. Nonetheless, fun colors to enhance your boring existence would be included. (This is not a black-and-white world, although it could be if you wanted it to be.)

Then, to provide the proper emotional crutch, the work of the artists and recorder would be taken by a musical conductor. He would write an original score and direct a thirty-piece orchestra with all the glorious sound that heightens and illuminates what is being seen. Filling out the sound would be all the bells, whistles, slams and bangs heard along the way, suitably improved upon to give the right punch. Yes, even the most mundane of twenty-three-minute lives would stand up. Sound unbelievable?

Well, that is this writer's attempt at giving you an idea of what it takes to complete one animated show. In actuality, it's even more complicated than that. All told, it takes about 400 people creating some 20,000 to 23,000 individual drawings, backed up by music and soundtracks, to do one twenty-three-minute episode of our show! And that, my friend, is one hell of a lot of ink and paint!

Originally our show was produced at Klasky Csupo on Highland Avenue, in Hollywood, but before it moved there it was a little further east on Seward Street in the building that produced the old *Beany and Cecil Show*. For reasons that I am not privy to, in the fourth season, the show switched to Film Roman in North Hollywood, where it has been produced ever since.

The first step in visual production is the storyboard process. Although Walt Disney never took credit for it himself, the concept was born out of his studio. Used by many, from Disney to Spielberg, storyboarding is an efficient tool for mapping out exactly the story being told and how that story will look. Okay, class, open your storyboards and follow along. As you can see, it is much like a Sunday comic strip, only much longer and in simple pencil on paper. And despite the fact that you know nothing about this tall tale, you can "read" it by glancing at the pictures in order.

Underneath each rough-penciled, panel-by-panel illustration, you will find a terse description or a piece of dialogue that marries the image with what is being said. And, put that eraser down! It's not supposed to be perfect!

The storyboard artist reads the script thoroughly before he starts drawing. He comes to fully understand the basic premise for the episode. He also has the overall concept and style of the series in mind. He knows what angles to use on Homer's belly. He knows to the core of his being the most attractive side to Marge's 'do, to Lisa's sax, to Bart's buns. He gets the first crack at mocking up the overall look for the animation director of that show.

Who are these guys? Besides being princes in my book, they are good cartoonists with the ability to make funny and expressive poses. This is no small task—they have to work fast and have the viewpoint of a director at the same time. They need to have the skills of an on-camera director, as these "comic book drawings" will illustrate not only the plot of the story but also the camera angles, the group shots, the close-ups, etc., that are inspired by the script. Unlike a live-action film that shoots all the different angles, the storyboard cuts right to the chase. The scene is "cut," so to speak, as it is first drawn. "Let's have Homer in a close-up when he runs through this plateglass window." "Yeah, then let's pull out and have a medium-shot of him falling down the flight of stairs ... a four-bump fall with the fifth bump landing him in the wagon." "Good. Then we'll pan with him, out the door, and pull up into a crane shot, out into the street. Cut to the bus going eighty miles per hour, then *bam!*" You got it.

The completed storyboard package is about 200 pages thick, with each page containing about four or five individual drawings. This valuable tool has become so universal that not only is it done in animation but it is now common practice in live-action film-making and commercials. Way to go, Walt!

Okay, so the script has been approved and is now in the hands of the six or so storyboard artists at Film Roman. They divide it among themselves with each one taking an act. "I want Act Three!" "No, *I* want Act Three!" "What you need is a pencil up your . . ." Okay, not really. This is a *work* environment, people! Professionals only need apply. But two of the "boys" remind me of frat brothers, belonging to Simpson Sigma Chi. Brad Abelson and Orlando Baeza kid and chide each other relentlessly, each one outdoing the other. Their office is like a dorm room, decorated personally, with all their funky paraphernalia including surfer photos framed in bamboo, tiki torches, a stand-up Pamela Anderson cut-out with Marge's blue hair and lots of "naked Bart butts" in various positions.

At this point in the artwork, changes are easily made and there is little detail—just an image of Homer, a suggestion of motion. They can put Mr. Eraser to work and simply remove the panels that don't work and/or add ones to remedy the scene. "Let's add some props on the steps." "How about some of Lisa's things at the top? A Malibu Stacy Dream House, her car and her pony? The vibrations could knock the pony into the car and have it crash into the house, smashing it." "Yeah, then he bounces by a pile of Maggie's pacifiers that are set up in perfect formation . . . knocking them over." "No, how about the other way around? They are just piled there and when he bounces by, all the pacifiers bounce into a perfect pyramid-shaped stack?" "Great . . ." If this doesn't sound like a fun gig you need a long vacation.

Jim Reardon is the current supervising animation director. He oversees all the other animation directors. Jim has been in charge for several years and has the unenviable task of deciding who gets to direct what episode. He is to the animators what the show runner is to the whole show. He is the head-honcho, the guy-in-charge, the kemo sabe, the autocrat of animation, the hero or the goat, depending on whether it looks good or looks rotten. Jim is a pretty easygoing guy, right down to the clips on his red suspenders. He sort of resembles an animated character, with his curly chin hairs and his round, rosy cheeks. Don't be fooled, though, he's all pro. His job is to "direct the directors . . . keep them in line." He also works with Gracie Productions, making sure that all parties are satisfied. Aaaaaand, he still manages to take the helm as director at least one show a season. I'd say the guy's probably not busy enough!

He decides who gets to direct what on a rotating basis, making sure that the assignments are spread out. This is not an enviable job. Seniority is a factor in the decision-making process and perhaps he makes the tough choices over a beer at a Moe's of his own personal choice. Or at least I'd hope so. There are about a dozen animation directors and they have various and sundry backgrounds. The title pretty much tells it all. A handful have reached this lofty position after having started out on the ground floor, so to speak, moving up from "background cleanup." This position, by the by, isn't even around anymore. So, where will those future directors come from? Film Roman has the reputation of helping animators out and encouraging artists to grow and develop.

One staff member, in particular, was responsible for most of this generosity. Phyllis Craig was the color key supervisor, in charge of overseeing the color design for all characters and background, but her real passion was in mentoring the young animators seeking employment and a chance in the biz. She was one of those people who everyone absolutely adored because she was so incredibly giving, of her time and her talent. She had been around for a long time, having started out with Disney. She had a keen ability to hone in on that one student who didn't necessarily have the training or the skill, but had the passion to work. She would encourage and nurture that artist, taking him or her to a whole new awareness and aptitude.

Phyllis was one of the founding members of Women in Animation, a nonprofit organization. The group's purpose is to foster a sense of dignity and address the career concerns women have in any and all aspects of the art and industry of animation. She put her actions where her heart was and has been justifiably honored with a scholarship fund in her name. Sadly, she passed away a few years ago, but Phyllis Craig was indeed a rare gem.

When Martin Scorsese directed *Cape Fear,* he shot for several months and covered every scene from all angles: a master—just shooting the whole scene with the camera in one spot, like you're watching a play; a close-up—making Robert DeNiro's nose about six feet tall; a two-shot—just on DeNiro and Jessica Lange; and an over-the-shoulder—zeroing in on Juliette Lewis, for example. When Rich Moore directed the parody "Cape Feare" on *The Simpsons*, he had to have a full understanding of filmmaking and the Scorsese style, but all in the spirit of animation. Our directors know the look of *E.T.* or *Gone With the Wind* or *The Wizard of Oz*. They understand how to guide the animation so it gives the suggestion of Hitchcock's *Vertigo* or so that it establishes a paranoia reminiscent of John Huston's *Treasure of the Sierra Madre*. Parodies of *King Kong, Citizen Kane, Thelma and Louise* and dozens of other film and television references have been intricately woven into the fabric of *The Simpsons*. A director's knowledge includes a well-rounded understanding of camera angles, lighting, wardrobe and especially—pause for effect—timing!

The animation director will work the storyboard to his satisfaction and then send the whole deal over to Gracie Films, the production company that produces the show in association with 20th-Century Fox Television. Here, the exec producer, and/or another producer, will study it and make notes. Since this is all rough, it's easy to change. "I think Nelson should use both fists to pound Bart." "Have Milhouse's glasses get fogged over." Things like this. It is, of course, the sincere hope of the animation director that they will *love* this storyboard.

MEANWHILE, back at Film Roman, they will have received the voice-track that we "laid down" (put on tape) at Fox. This tape will have been edited to about twelve to fifteen minutes of sequential dialogue. The animation director and his assistant now have to figure out how much time they have for each scene. More dialogue means less time for nonverbal action. And leave us not forget: What's the most important thing about comedy? Timing! It may take 1.5 seconds to have Mr. Burns look at his distorted face in a brandy glass, or three seconds to have Marge make a determined approach on the bowling lane. Thank God for stopwatches and mirrors.

Once the notes come back from Gracie, the storyboard guys polish it up and we say good-bye to Brad (or any of the five other storyboarders) for this show. The done deal is then routed to the layout artists. These magicians will create the key artwork that will become the episode itself, but they need more than the storyboard to do their work.

Squeezing by the file cabinets that hold all the show's props, background and character designs from the third season on (no wonder there is no smoking in the building!) you enter the hub of the design department. Each designer has his own space, usually surrounded by personal photos and artwork. A couple of curious mementos dot the place: a hanging Oriental fish, a black velvet painting of Yogi Bear circa 1960 and, on one wall, a huge map of the United States. Over the years about seventy employees of Film Roman have identified their hometowns and labeled them with their names beside that city. From Alaska to Massachusetts and 3,000 miles of "Springfield" in between, these guys have tons of imagination. After all, we are counting on them to come up with the complete look of the show.

The character designer's work impacts the layout artist because he or she has the task of creating any new characters for that particular episode. *The Simpsons* has introduced a whole new look for animation that was never done before. During the first season, David Silverman and Wes Archer were the directors who set the design for the characters. Doing the transition from *The Tracey Ullman Show* bumpers to the half-hour series was very difficult in terms of the animation. The stiff, angular shapes were much too difficult to duplicate en masse, so David and Wes set the standard. Our character designers take that developed look and extend it to the guest characters on the show. They give "the Simpson touch" to Suzanne Somers, Bob Hope and Gary Coleman, as well as the assorted jurors, kids, parents and other extras on the show. They have to be designed to the Groening standard. You can imagine the challenge when it came to designing Jay Leno. How do you design Jay Leno when the whole look of *The Simpsons* is *chinless*? Matt, who has always run a tight ship regarding the quality of the show, still checks all the designs to make sure they are within the style that he created.

Our designers take great pride in the amount of research that they do in order to be as specific as possible. They pick up a broad education researching every new challenge. Just what would Dr. Nick Riviera's operating room, located at the Springfield Mall, next to Gum for Less and two doors down from I Can't Believe It's a Law Firm, look like? Ah! Everything you need to know is on *ER*! The leggy nurse's assistant will be wearing the latest in V-neck hospital green and the surgeon will clutch state-of-the-art medical tools enhanced by the artist's pen and sicko imagination.

The background designers come up with the whole scenic look of the show. In the beginning, there was no consistency in the animation. Matt did all the artwork himself and because the bumpers were, by nature, individual stories, this style was never considered "problematic." But when the series was born, the locations and the looks of the characters kept changing from show to show, causing much confusion. "Wait a second, wasn't there a wall there last week? She's walking through a wall!" David and Wes came up with model sheets in order to set a design standard. They clearly defined the layout of the house, inside and out, and they figured out just exactly how many points are on Bart's head. These blueprints set the standard. (He has nine.)

Parody requires research. The writers will drop some silly or poignant visual joke that the animators have to execute. The animator doesn't make up the idea but will enhance the joke through his or her design choices. Some of the most difficult visual jokes are found in signage and marquees. Sharp fans always have their eyes open for the latest turn of phrase. Stores at the Springfield Mall include International House of Answering Machines, The Jerkey Hut (conducting a "Sausage Sale!") and The Ear Piercery. Marquees on Broadway read, "Tommy Tune in Gotta Mince!," "David Copperfield's Astonishing Girlfriend!" and "Hoofin' 'n' Mouthin'." It can take a good two hours for the writers to come up with one of these ideas—and much, much longer to get the design just right. The designers know these gems are part of the strength of the show and, even though they only appear on screen for less than a passing glance, they will eventually be captured on videotape and replayed over and over again by the more fanatical of beer-chugging *Simpsons* lovers.

Occasionally, the design team will take a field trip, after turning in their parental consent forms. A bunch of them went to Disneyland to observe the layout of The Happiest Place on Earth for the "Itchy and Scratchy Land" show. Thus, they knew the Disney look when designing signs depicting which rides weren't in operation: Head Basher, Blood Bath, Mangler and the Nurses Station. Another time, the whole department got to go to a local bowling alley to get just the right look for "Team Homer." Lance Wilder in Background got to scope out the size, shape and style of the facility; Jeff Weekly in Props got to check out and sketch the props for the show: the pins, the shoes and even the hand-dryers so the viewers could "feel the warm air"; and Joe Wack, the supervisor for the character designs, got to check out the "cast of characters" that frequent this type of venue. Pop quiz: What kind of humanoids hang out in a bowling alley, sorry, Bowling *Centre*, at two o'clock in the afternoon on a workday? (Pause for image.) Yeah, that's what they saw too. (Actually, it occurs to me that most bowling enthusiasts are also *Simpsons* fans, and since you have purchased this book you are a *Simpsons* fan and thus a bowler. In fact, you are probably reading this right now between frames while your team loses once again to Jiffy Lube West. . . . Uh-oh, I fear I have alienated my readership. Well, go iron your bowling shirt and work on your handicap!) The designers got to watch someone just like you tilt a brew and throw a gutterball— *while getting paid!* Cool. Knock down a few pins, take a few photos . . . not a bad gig! Of course, field trips are few and far between, so, in a pinch, they turn to cyberspace. Convenient, but I bet they miss the sound of a clean strike!

Hats off to the prop guys. And to the background artists—
take a break at a nearby lake or mall or in a community room on
a deserted island. And to the character designers, here's lookin'
atcha, baby!

YOU leave any semblance of a private office behind as you step out
into the room where Springfield comes to life. Judging by the surroundings you wouldn't be surprised to sit down to talk to a
bargain-basement tax consultant. Gray partitions form spaces in
the drop-ceilinged room in which highly trained artists are expected to shine. There are no windows. How do you bring life to
fluorescent lights and blank walls? You tape construction paper
up at a clever angle to direct the flickering glow down on your
desktop and you cover the Sheetrock with Dragonslayer posters—
at least if you are layout artist Paul Wee, you do. You highlight
the gaps with some of your most inspired movie banners, those of
busty wenches preferably, that you've designed for your film
school pals in your spare time. With that little bit of visual stimulation you sit down to make magic.

This is a select crew of from six to eight artists who are
trained in fine art, but, unfortunately for the Smithsonian, were
raised on *The Flintstones*. Their detailed work requires they know
how a body moves, bends, twists and responds, even a rather odd
body like Homer's. Let's see, in "Bart the Daredevil" . . . Ah, he's
falling down the side of a mountain. This will be fun! The artists
are, essentially, the cinematographers of animation. They have the
challenging task of keeping the visual dynamics of the

scenes in mind—the movement, the emotion and, uh, like I said before, the timing.

So, here is the skinny: The animation director divvies up the show among the layout artists, giving each about twenty scenes to draw. They, in turn, take the storyboard and expand on it by making individual drawings of the key scenes. These are hand-drawn onto 9 × 12 white paper with absolute accuracy and creative expertise. Each drawing is held in place by three little pegs on the animation light board. The light shines from under a glass plate so the artist can trace most of his previous work. Then, by making a slight change in the part that is moving, the illusion of movement is created. By "flipping" back and forth from page to page, the artist can check and double-check his accuracy. These become the actual basis for the images that we see on Sunday night at eight. The layout artists, when confronted with a unique pose or expression, will use a mirror and "become" a particular emotion. Okay, raise your hand if you've ever done this. Right, but I'll hazard a guess you weren't being paid. The artist will sit with a headset on and listen to the voice-track. The intensity, power, emotion are all carried through the voice. These vocal qualities cue them as to which perspective is "right." They will take any number of angles or distances on the characters. You want to see tonsils in a scream? No problem. They can magnify or warp whatever background was provided and magically convert the storyboard into a full-on scene. If you can picture an animator with a mirror in one hand and a handheld tape recorder in the other, you can just imagine how it would look to see one of them doing his best to capture the drunken look on Groundskeeper Willie's face. In a gray cubicle they hoist a bottle of water, pinch an eye shut and pretend they're chugging back a bottle of liquid courage on the sly. With all the creative power they can muster, they will take on the Captain's seafarin' expression as he's saying, "Aahrr! I'll gut you like an endangered whale!" Then, image in mind, they turn to the paper and lay it down. The artist will work the scene, listening, drawing, rewinding and listening again, and again and again. By the time the layout artist has completed his work, I lay odds that he hears those lines wandering through his dreams. "Ow! Quit it! Ow! Quit it! Ow! Quit it."

Following the animation director's approval of the layout, the animator will take the drawings and add frames to expand and connect the scenes. It begins to look like a somewhat jumpy and schizo episode at this point. They have their own stack of 9×12s, and continue with the flip technique already started by the layout artist. It is extremely time consuming but that, folks, is what animation is all about. With no bones, no muscles, no organs, these inanimate drawings need life. A little latent acting ability is a plus, and, admit it, who on planet earth doesn't think they can act? I'm really sorry I don't have any of this on video; it would be better than William Shatner doing "Mister Tambourine Man." But, with the dialogue track playing in the background, like some kind of perverse disco, you can catch them on their feet from time to time. With belly thrust out and chin pulled in, they work that mirror, baby! Maybe this is truly necessary, maybe, or maybe this is what fluorescent lights and no windows for ten hours a day do to a person.

In order to accommodate the director, there is an assistant director. Together, they will work out the timing. To do this, the drawings are photographed with an animation camera that is connected to a computer. Yes, you knew it was coming, computers. While *The Simpsons* is done almost entirely by hand, somewhat of a dinosaur in the present-day animation scene, the team has succumbed to the allure of technology in certain areas. At the bottom edge of the camera stand are those same pegs that hold the 9 × 12s in place. This is extremely important. If one weren't careful one could overlap two images. "Um . . . what is Homer doing to Santa's Little Helper? I didn't think that was legal in Springfield."

When all the drawings have been photographed in order, they add the sound track and, voilà!—you have a very basic, black-and-white animated video called an animatic. This is one of the most important tools used in the production of the show. It's also a hoot to watch! Although the animation is still rough at this point, the animatic is like a mini-movie and gives the director an idea of what's working. "I'm not laughing. It needs . . . timing!"

There is an opening night of sorts when the animatic, the culmination of weeks of hard work, is shown to the powers that be at Gracie. After viewing the animatic, the writer/producers tend to ask for more specific content rather than removing or completely changing a scene. This is what the animation director wants, loves. Sure, he'll be happy with a request for a new angle here or there, a better joke in Act Two, but not the horror of major reworking of the animation. A statement like, "Act Three really doesn't work that way," will strike terror into their delicate hearts.

Assuming all goes pretty well with the animatic, and our animation director doesn't need a transfusion, a few changes are made and approved and all the drawings are transferred to acetate celluloids, or more commonly, cels. *The Simpsons* does each and every one of these by hand. Once these are complete, they are shipped off to Korea to be Xeroxed and painted, but I am getting ahead of myself.

The sheet timer, Lindsey Pollard, dictates the exact internal timing of each scene, including blinks, head turns, hand movements, walking across the room, falling down a well and speeding off into the sunset. She will write down how many frames it takes to get from one position to the next, establishing how long the camera will hold onto each frame and consequently each moment, before moving onto the next. It takes a subtle sense of timing and an expertise in math skills. Because the timing is dictated by so many frames per second, the challenge isn't in the big stuff, as would be expected, but rather in the dramatic or sad moments that will help to determine the emotional response from the viewer. Sensitivity and a love for minutiae is the key.

The lip assignment guy (can you believe that name?!) has the task of determining the shape of Milhouse's mouth when he is saying, "My dad's a pretty big wheel down at the cracker factory," or how many different lip positions to give Cletus when he says, "Hey Ma, look at that pointy-haireded [sic] little girl!" There are sixteen stock mouth shapes in all and the challenge is to note the exact mouth positions, one through sixteen, as the characters speak. What an amazing gig and what a fun thing to share with your grandkids someday . . . "I was the lip assignment guy on *The Simpsons* for twenty-six years!"

Color! Color! Color! Karen Bauer-Riggs, Anne Balser, Amy Klees Rychlick and Syd Kato sit at computers in a room with, yes, windows! They are surrounded by rainbows, funky Barbies, Chinese hanging lamps, tons of family photos, bamboo on the walls, *Speed Racer* and *Ultra Man* posters—no office would be complete without those—and a token ceramic pig. To step from the black-and-white world of pencil where the show has been growing into this sanctuary of color is a remarkable experience. Being a gal who knows color coordination, I couldn't help but notice that each of the four gals in that department represented a different season of the year, making for a very, excuse me, colorful package indeed. (P.S. I'm a spring.)

This color department, using PhotoShop, chooses what colors go where, for characters, props, backgrounds—*everything*. After the whole show has been drawn, a color is assigned to that item. The colors are number-coded and marked on the clean drawings. They only have 200 colors to choose from, whereas an animated feature or one of the new TV series done in computer might have a selection of 2,000, actually an infinite selection of tones and shades. Going digital would be a big shift because *The Simpsons* is hand-painted (which I'll explain later) with special colors that were decided on twelve years ago. It is a dinosaur in this department as well. If they were to go digital, which no one wants (or anyone who does isn't talking), they would have an un-limited number of choices. But what would you do with all that premixed paint over in Korea? "Hey, if it ain't broke . . ." Given such a small palette, the challenge is obvious. The subtleties are what make the show so unique, so you can imagine that the more training a color designer has, the more we will all benefit. Strong in art backgrounds, all these women are skilled in understanding the composition of color, geometric design and the integration of both.

For example, one particular challenge was in one of the very first episodes, "Bart the Genius," when Bart is visualizing a math problem. "At seven-thirty A.M. an express train traveling sixty miles an hour leaves Santa Fe bound for Phoenix . . ." The scene dissolves to Bart's visualization of the problem. Bart sees himself standing near the doors, looking down the length of the car. Superimposed is the equation "40 divided by 8=," then over the heads of each of the passengers in the car appear the numbers 1, 2, 3, 4, 5, etc. This particular scene was done in black and white. What a challenge for the color department. The subtleties that they chose, the shades of grays, the offs of whites, the shading . . . so effective. And the numbers in Bart's mind were then colored in pink to make them stand out. Just the idea of using black and white in a medium that depends so much on color is a creative departure—it is refreshing. The ladies in color love to tell the tale of the guy who came in and worked for a few weeks until they discovered he was color blind! His work was . . . unusual. "So, you're using that shade of blue on Bart's face . . . why, exactly?" He, uh, didn't think it would be a problem. Sounds like Homer got loose at Film Roman.

Typically, there are seven or eight shows in various stages of development by midseason. The animation of the shows has to overlap or they would never get the job done. (You can imagine the entire crew hovering over the layout artist waiting for him to finish the scene so they can run it off to the next step.) For example, come July, there will be two shows in animation, three in final timing, one in animatic, one recording, three in layout and two in storyboards. Film Roman is one poppin' studio!

When a show's development is completed at Film Roman it is still far from a completed show. The package consists of key artwork, showing poses and backgrounds, new props and costumes. It includes detailed timing sheets that operate as a blueprint and the paint-by-numbers work of the color department. But it's still a few frames short, just a hint of the smooth final product that will air. It is now ready for the big final step, Korea.

WHILE computer and digital technology are slowly taking over most of the animation industry, *The Simpsons* remains 100 percent hand-painted. Did you get that—100 percent *hand-painted!* If you consider that it takes anywhere from fifteen to twenty-four pieces of art for every *second* that you see on the screen and that the show is anywhere from twenty-one to twenty-three minutes long—we are talking somewhere between 18,900 and 33,220 hand-painted cels per episode! This attention to detail and the continual use of actual artists instead of computers makes *The Simpsons* the leader in this rapidly emerging industry.

But we can only make this claim by acknowledging the amazing overseas team that makes it possible. The painting is done in Korea or, quite frankly, it would never happen. It would be too expensive. I'm sure that there are thousands of young artists who could paint cels here in the U.S. of A. but not for a couple dollars an hour. So, Film Roman's detailed set-up artwork and exposure sheets fly over the Pacific to Korea.

When the shipment first arrives in Korea, the exposure sheets have to first be translated into Korean. Then the work is divided up and distributed to the staff. They have exactly the same character and background model sheets as we do and all the tools they need to do the job. There, a team of unsung heroes draws all the in-between poses and copies them to cels, and then another team flips them over and, using the paint-by-number instructions of the color department, paints what we see on some future Sunday evening. Then, on to the camera room to shoot the frame-by-frame twenty-plus minutes of animation. Akom, the overseas animation studio, has about seven to eight weeks to do this and get the finished product back to Film Roman.

Once back on American soil, the animation director, who is well into his next show, sits with the editor and watches the overseas work and takes note of what needs to be fixed. Any clean-up or rewriting takes place here. Our producers have about five weeks to do any retakes, ADR or any further editing. Chances are that the show is too long and some of the scenes originally animated get cut—boo-hoo. There is also a little leeway with the opening credits. Ever notice that Bart sometimes takes a little "shortcut" on his skateboard in the opening credits? That's because the show came out a little long and it was too good to cut, so we had to compensate for the overtime by cutting back somewhere. The opening was cleverly designed just for this purpose. The network has very strict regulations about how

long every show can be and let us not forget that the whole purpose of television is to get you to buy detergent, cars and Poké-
mon. So when you include the opening titles of the show and the
closing credits, we're talkin' twenty-one minutes—and not a second more, dammit!

The "Mickster"

▶ **SEPTEMBER 12, 1994**

*W*e are already on show number seventeen for the season! Can't
believe how fast the weeks fly by. *This particular episode,
"Radioactive Man," has Mickey Rooney flying in to convince Milhouse that "you have to do this. If not for yourself, then for the
moviegoing public, and for the foreign markets." And to think it
was only fifty-five years ago that he was saying the same thing to
Judy Garland! We were all anticipating his arrival. In the meantime, we just kept recording. He wasn't in the show until the very
last scene so it didn't matter that he wasn't there yet. Come one
o'clock, we broke for lunch. Still no Mick.*

*After lunch, we started scene six. Suddenly, the door
opened and in walked—a production assistant. "Mickey is*

on his way," he blurted. "He's stuck in traffic." Just then, as if on cue, the door swung open and in strutted Mickey Rooney, all five-foot three-inches of him! Definitely someone I could relate to.

"Hello, everyone!" he said in that voice that is robust, full-of-life and rarin' to go. "The Mickster has arrived!"

What timing! Suddenly I had the urge to grab a broom and start sweepin' the place. "Come on, you guys, let's put on a show!"

Mickey was exhilarating. I think he has something like thirty children, so it doesn't surprise me the guy is so full of pep. Here is this living legend who started working when he was barely three years old and who hasn't stopped since.

What is really cool is that you get a guy like Mickey Rooney, who has probably had every opportunity in the world to become cynical, jaded and totally disaffected to this industry, and he is none of those things. Instead, here he is, seventy years old and still kickin'! I think that is pretty darn commendable. He has no ego. Actually, I take that back. He is pure ego, but I don't mean in a stuck-up sort of way. He has all the confidence that "ego" implies, but he backs it up with a tongue-in-cheek attitude about himself. He has no doubts about what an incredibly powerful guy he is, and it doesn't come off as a facade. This guy is so full of himself, yet so willing to make fun, that once he got going, it was impossible to stop him! He was overflowing with confidence, certainty and personal power—he had no fear.

We started the record. The scene has a helicopter flying in

with Mickey Rooney gracefully jumping into Bart's treehouse. Milhouse is there too.

MICKEY:

(VERY OUT OF BREATH) Hi, Milhouse. The studio sent me to talk to you, being a former child star myself and the number-one box office draw from 1939 to 1940.

Mickey interrupted himself. "Did you all know that I was once the highest paid teenager in Hollywood? Of course, it's peanuts compared to what you all get today, but back then two hundred dollars a week was like robbin' the bank."

We all had a laugh and continued with the record.

MICKEY:

C'mon, Milhouse, you have to do this . . . for me, the Mickster.

He turned to us between takes. "Hey, did you know that Walt Disney named Mickey Mouse after me? It's true. Every bit of it. I was five years old and working on my Mickey McGuire comedies at Warner Bros. when a young Walt Disney introduced himself to me." There was no stopping him now and even the director just sat there waiting. "He showed me this picture of a character he had drawn and I told him what a good lookin' mouse it was. Well, Walt stopped for a second and just sat there

thinking. Then he turned to me and said, 'Tell me something, how would you like me to name this mouse after you?' And I said, 'I sure would like that, but right now I got to go and get a tuna sandwich.' And that is a true story." I believe him . . . Hey, what else could I do?

I suspect Mickey could have gone on and on all afternoon, and into the next day or week even with all his stories. He was so totally full of life and clearly loving the one he's having. Somehow, standing across from him and watching this pint-sized dynamo spew anecdotes of his vastly colorful life sort of reminded me of— how do I say this?—me! (I guess we have a little more in common than just our stature!) I couldn't help but think that he loves sharing the things that he has done just about as much as I do. I began to wonder if maybe Mickey might own a pink Miata, my personal shout of "Hey, here I am! Let the show begin!" I find it so darn admirable that he can ride over the wave, so to speak, and be himself within the tough Hollywood game. I hope I can do the same.

Everyone thoroughly enjoyed every last drop of Mickey Rooney. He burst onto the scene, stole the moment and continued to steal it until his part was in the can. He gave us a little soft-shoe and shuffled to the door saying, "Nice workin' with ya! Love the show!"

Off he went, tipping his hat as he was out the door. We all sat there in the wake of his performance, staring at the closed door behind him, wallowing in the after-glow of Mickey. I looked around at all the faces. Some were a little perplexed by the show they had just seen and some were just plain stunned. My mouth *was slightly open and I couldn't stop shaking my head. Suddenly, the door burst open again.*

"*Did I tell you about the time I nearly broke my two front teeth by flying in a harness that snapped over a crowd of people in the dead of winter? It was with Judy in* Babes on Broadway. *You see, it was Christmas time . . .*"

Spartacus!

► OCTOBER 17, 1995

I got called into the studio for a separate session today. There was nothing particularly special about it, no biggie, except for the fact that Kirk Douglas *was meeting me there to do his scene! Ho-hum.* I'm suuure! Omygod! *I mean, really, what does one say to a man who has earned the highest civilian award ever given in the United States, the Presidential Medal of Freedom? Then there are his American Cinema Award, the German Golden Kamera Award, the National Board of Review's Career Achievement Award, three Best Actor nominations for the Oscar and Best Actor winner by the New York Film Critics Circle for* Lust for Life. *(I know—I looked it up!) I knew that he was coming, this was not a surprise. What* was *a total and complete surprise, was that I ended up <u>directing</u> Spartacus!*

At 11:07, a shiny black limo pulled into the studio's parking lot. Okay, I was watching. The door opened, no waiting for the driver, and out stepped Mr. Douglas, dapper and full of beans. "This won't take long," he graveled to the chauffeur within. "So keep the car running." Coming from the actor that defined selfish, cocky, intense and powerful, Champion *in 1949, this seemed right in character. I ducked out of sight.*

The script, "The Day the Violence Died," was another gem. Kirk was our guest, playing the role of Chester Lampwick, a man who claims that Roger Meyers, Sr. (Alex Rocco), stole the Itchy character from him.

We went into Studio B where our stands and script pages were already set up. I put on my headset and looked over at Mr. D, who was waving the headset in his hands like a crazed parking attendant waving a flashlight. "I'm not wearing these things. They hurt my ears." He tossed them on the table. Go, Kirk! I looked through the glass at Josh Weinstein, director with a big problem! He was in the sound booth, a place where sound only travels via microphones and . . . headsets! He shot me a look of desperation. His shoulders were bunched up around his ears and he wore an expression that reminded me, for some reason, of a grade schooler showing up without his homework—"My dog ate it." Ironically, he looked absolutely adorable. I suppressed a giggle, difficult as that was under the circumstances. I realized very quickly that there was no way he was gonna pull this off solo. Somehow we were going to have to work together. The problem was that I couldn't even inconspicuously hand-signal to Josh that everything was okay. We both just sort of looked at each other and

threw caution to the wind. In my headset I am hearing, "Uh, get a level."

So, right after his look (drumroll, please), Nancy to the rescue! I had no time to think, saying, "Uh . . . yeah, sure, no problem, that's fine, Mr. Douglas. They just need to get a level from you." He looked at me, a little curious. I went on: "Uh . . . good . . . fine . . . Just start at the top and read a couple of lines." He did and I checked with Bob, the engineer. All was A-OK. "All right," I continued. "Let's lay this puppy down." Eat your heart out, James Cameron.

"Okay," he replied. "But I'm only giving you two takes and then I'm outta here."

Omygod! Nothing like a no-pressure job! Suddenly I got a strange sensation that the whole show was counting on me to pull this thing off! It's all in your hands, Nancy. If you blow this, you're banished from Springfield forever! I bought some time by carefully adjusting my own headset. Josh's voice came through crystal clear. "We only need one good take, Nancy." He didn't have to say, "Please!" I could hear it in his voice. I watched Mr. Douglas eyeball his script. *Omygod, girl . . . what are you doing?* kept repeating itself in my mind. *If you screw this up . . . so much for your directing debut.*

I took a deep breath and smiled at Mr. Douglas. "Uh . . . two takes? No problem, sir. We'll have you out of here in no time. So let's just take it from the top of the page and we'll do the scene a couple times and then you're on your way."

And we were off!

BUM:

He stole the character from me in 1928. When I complained, his thugs kicked me out of his office and dropped an anvil on me. Luckily, I was carrying an umbrella at the time. When I got out of the hospital the following summer, I had no friends, no money, and part of an umbrella lodged in my back. Whatever you do, don't touch this button.

BART:

You invented Itchy? The Itchy & Scratchy *Itchy?*

BUM:

Sure. In fact, I invented the whole concept of cartoon violence. Before I came along, all cartoon animals did was play the ukulele. I charged all that.

BART:

Well, I'm not calling you a liar, but . . . (Beat) I can't think of a way to finish that sentence.

BUM:

So I'm a liar, am I?

He had another line or two but I wasn't really listening. He had flubbed. Everything would have been just perfectly perfect

except instead of saying "I changed *all that*" he said, "I charged *all that.*" *I know. I know! It totally does not make any sense, unless you account for the fact that unless Kirk does the next take perfectly, I may be "charged" with treason! Kirk eyed his watch and looked at me. Well, Ms. Director? We only had one more take! And the limo was waiting!*

I glanced at Josh. *He was pacing the booth with ants in his shoes, poor guy.* I turned to Kirk and said, "That was excellent, sir . . . uh, . . . brilliant. Just give us another one and on that second speech let's really hear how proud you are changing *all that.*" *Okay, not the most brilliant direction of all time but, hey, I'm sweatin' bullets here! He stared at me for a moment. I waited for him to answer me—say anything! Maybe Mr. Douglas isn't used to being directed by a chick. From my headset I am hearing Josh,* "Okay, good . . . you're doing good. Let's keep our fingers crossed."

Kirk nodded.

"Whenever you're ready, sir."

I wiped the sweat from my brow—this directing stuff is hard work—and we started again. Kirk was cruising. Everything was going along just swimmingly, when he got to the infamous line. I held my breath.

BUM:

Before I came along, all cartoon animals did was play the ukulele. I charged all that.

"Charged" again? My mind is racing, *What the hell are we going to do now? He is out of here in less than one minute and we didn't get a clean take! Now what?*

Well, there was only one thing left to do: I let out a huge, fake sneeze, interrupting Mr. Douglas and splashing my script with the evidence. I was not about to be the goat.

"Omygosh!" I said, pretending to wipe snot from my nose. "Excuse me! I totally ruined your read. I am so sorry."

Kirk looked a little stunned. "That's all right," he said. "No biggie."

By now, Josh was picking his jaw up off the floor! My mind was screaming. *No biggie! No biggie! Kirk Douglas said, "No biggie!" I Love him!*

"Uh, great. So . . . let me see, let's just start with your line: 'Before I came along, all cartoon animals did was play the ukulele. I changed *all that.*' And continue to the end."

Josh, by now, was nowhere to be seen. I thought he might have fainted, but later he insisted that he merely dropped his pencil. Keeping my fingers and my toes crossed, we did it one more time.

BUM:

Before I came along, all cartoon animals did was play the ukulele. I changed all that . . .

He went on to the end flawlessly! "Aaaaand, cut! That's the take. Perfect!" (I always wanted to say that.) I was about to give Kirk a "high-five"—I was so pleased at what we had accomplished. Instead, I reined myself in and settled for a simple, "Pleasure working with you, Mr. Douglas."

And now I am going to update my resumé.

The Snap, Crackle and Pop

At this point in time, the script has been written, recorded and fully animated. It has gone to Korea and back again—possibly several times. Changes have been made. Scenes have been eliminated and scenes have been added. It is two weeks before the show is supposed to air but something is missing. *Where's the music?* Gotta love pressure.

This is where Alf Clausen comes in. It all starts on a Friday afternoon at a music-spotting session. Alf, our music composer, Chris Ledesma, music editor, along with the executive producer and a couple other producers, "spot" the right places for the music and decide on the overall style of each piece. Notes will be taken at this meeting resulting in a breakdown of music cues. These indicate how long each piece is and describe what is needed.

From here on, it gets pretty complicated. As with the work on the exposure sheets in the animation department, math skills are an absolute necessity! Each of the musical cues has to be broken into seconds and hundredths of seconds to time out with each line of dialogue, each piece of action and each cut from scene to scene so Alf can have a "book" of timing notes. This book can be anywhere from thirty to fifty pages, depending on how complicated the score is.

Once this book is compiled, Alf and his orchestrator work together to prepare the music for the orchestra. Some of the more intense episodes, like "Treehouse of Horror" and "A Streetcar Named Marge," will take a considerably longer time due to the sheer number of cues. It is all Alf can do to just get the cues composed, so his orchestrator prepares the orchestral scores from Alf's sketches.

A week later, with the music all laid out, Alf is on the conductor's podium with baton in hand, and the thirty-five-piece orchestra is at the ready! Rumor has it that Alf taught Mr. Largo, the band leader for Springfield Elementary School, everything he knows.

In "Who Shot Mr. Burns?" Tito Puente guest starred as himself. Here you have these two incredible conductor-musicians in what could have been a face-off of power. Tito walked in the door and turned to the first person he met. "Where is Alf Clausen?" This person replied, "I'm Alf." A little surprised, Tito said, "What I want to know first is, am *I* going to tell *you* what to do or are *you* going to tell *me* what to do?" Alf, used to dealing with me, said without dropping a beat, "Well, I'm a really good listener."

And to that, Tito replied, "All right, *you* tell *me* what to do." Obviously Mr. Largo isn't the only one who benefited from Alf.

Part of the challenge Alf faces is how to make the parodies sound like the songs they emulate. This is the genius of Alf. In "Simpsoncalifragilisticexpiala-d'oh-cious," he had the task of creating a sound that felt like and reminded you of the popular *Mary Poppins* hit, but was just tongue-in-cheek enough so that it didn't get us sued. He goes to great lengths to figure out the original songs' harmonies, melodies, rhythms and orchestrations so that he can then "tweak" this and "sweeten" that and otherwise shift it enough so that this new song reminds the listener, but is still unique.

This musical team is like icing on the Simpsons' cake. A very loyal union of artists, most of them have worked on the show since the beginning.

To get an idea of the range of musical styles in *The Simpsons*, listen to *Songs in the Key of Springfield* and *Go Simpsonic with the Simpsons*—nothing like a little bit of shameless self-promotion. Ranging from musical comedy to country and everything in between, Alf has managed to get two prestigious Emmy awards along with twelve—count 'em, twelve!—nominations!

In addition to composing the musical underscore, Alf also writes all the original songs for the show. The lyrics come from the writers, but it is up to Alf to weave in the different styles. He gets the script pages with the lyrics on them and from there he writes the songs. On *The Simpsons,* it is never done the other way 'round. Alf will turn the song concepts into musical tracks. Chris Ledesma will then take a temp track (short for "temporary" as it will be replaced with the "real thing" later) of the song and joins the actors in a musical recording session. This is my most absolute favoritest part of the show. I love the singing. Chris is a complete and total joy to work with and never complains that Bart isn't the best vocalist of the century! I personally would love to see the future of *The Simpsons* on the big screen, doing a film that includes lots of music! What a hoot.

As with the dialogue record, we are all together in the studio. Occasionally someone will be missing and will be picked up solo, but it is ideal for all of us to be in the same room at the same time.

We listen through our headphones to a click track that clicks off the beats of the song. Once we get our cue, we start singing with the temp track. Once this recording is completed, it is mixed with the instrumental track, called a "composite," and then it is sent to the animators. And from there—you guessed it—it is animated. This is all done fairly early in the production. In fact, eight months later, when it is fully animated and we have to go in to do a little "clean up" on our singing, I have completely forgotten what we did! It is always such a surprise—"Wow, we sound pretty good!"

There is another area that deserves mentioning, and that is sound effects. These are the wonderful pops, snorts, burps, squishes, punches, flaps, whooshes and other sounds that put the chocolate sprinkles on the icing of *The Simpsons'* cake. Travis Powers is the man in charge and has been since the Tracey Ullman days. Over the years he has built himself a library of sounds enviable to any ten-year-old boy. Where most sound effects are typically created in a studio setting, Travis actually will go on location to get the real deal. OR . . . he will create the sound in his own backyard. For "Homer's Odyssey," Travis had the challenge of making the sound of a giant rock being dragged across the yard. So he got himself a giant rock, and at three in the morning dragged the thing around his backyard!

But what do you suppose he did to create the sound of the heart being ripped out of Bart's chest by his pubescent heartthrob baby-sitter (voiced by Sara Gilbert) in "New Kid on the Block"? He took a watermelon and cut a hole, about the size of his fist, in it. Then he recorded the sound of him punching his fist inside and squishing it around. The sssslllrrrppp you hear when Laura removes the heart is the actual sound of Travis removing his fist from inside the melon. To add depth to the overall effect, he layered that with sounds of celery strands being ripped from the stalk to emulate the muscles and tendons being ripped. Once Bart's heart is in her hand, you hear the beating of a drum sound being recorded in reverse, that is, the tape being played backward and recorded, giving it the "lub-dub lub-dub" sound. Then Travis took a slab of meat and threw it against the wall, just as Laura did to Bart's heart. It slides down the wall, while Travis records a wet hand pushed and dragged on a dry surface. It lands in the waste-basket, just as it did on-camera. *Ker-plop!*

All the door slamming—for real. All the tinkling ice at Moe's—for real. All the screeching of brakes and honking of horns—the real deal. I'd like to say that Maggie's pacifier sucking sound is really Travis doin' it for the sake of art, but actually it is a mouth effect that anyone can do.

I remember early on being asked to lay down a whole set of burps. In fact, all of us were asked. Of course, I volunteered very loudly because I take great pride in being one of the best belchers west of Moe's. Dan challenged me and, with Cokes in hand, we burped out a symphony of gastral explosions that evolved into a gastral explosion of another kind. Pretty soon, the whole lot of us were burping and mouth-farting until we cried. This was one of the most pleasurable moments on the show.

Travis says, "Sounds are like colors, and in particular, watercolors. You hear all the layers overlapping each other . . . It is also like music, layering one after another, creating a whole concerto of noises."

To give an example of how all these production elements come together, one of my favorite episodes is Matt Groening's "Colonel Homer." This script is delicious and you get a visual and aural feast with the episode. One scene takes place in a recording studio. The background designers must have gone on another field trip for this one because they really captured the look of your typical musical recording studio. Here you see the two separate rooms, one for the artist and the other for the engineer, with a pane of glass between them. The designers added their own special touch by putting a few extra cracks on the walls and designing a slightly dilapidated ceiling. You also cannot help but notice that the soundproofing on the walls is falling off. I am not sure what studio they visited, but I am sure they are out there somewhere— not only in the city of Springfield.

The prop designers had a field day with all the props: the studio "in-session" red light, the mixing board, the musical instruments, the volume-unit meters indicating how loud Lurleen was singing—right down to the picks on the guitarist's fingers. Beautiful detail.

And the color designers blended the muted oranges, mauves, tans, browns and grays in the studio, making them complement each other. Inside the engineer's booth, the colors were darker, but putting Homer in a white suit made him stand out and look even a little more goofy.

The character designers had fun creating the musicians and their cowboy hats, and really did a nice turn on the studio engineer, Mr. Boylan. You see, nine months earlier, the real Mr. Boylan produced *The Simpsons Sing the Blues*. It ended up selling over three million copies, rendering it a certified triple-platinum. Both Boylan and the character, which sort of looked like Boylan, had a pony-tail and round, wire-rimmed glasses. Just FYRP . . . for your reading pleasure.

The sound effects were in full gear in the opening scene. Homer and family go to the movies. While sitting there, you hear the sounds of Homer *slurping* a jumbo soft drink, but there's no soda left. He begins *sucking air* annoyingly. Then he takes the lid off the cup and lifts it up, trying to get the ice chips to fall into his mouth. He *taps* on the upturned bottom of the cup; and the ice comes *slowly plopping* out of the cup in one mushy chunk, *smattering* into his face. Of course, Homer chokes. Then, you hear his feet *sticking* and *unsticking* on the floor repeatedly. He *grabs* one handful of popcorn after another, dropping most of it on the floor. The whole scene was topped off with the audience *splattering* Homer with candy, food and other squishy things.

On the way home, Bart sums it all up. "Forget it, Mom. Dad's really mad. The tendons are throbbing at the base of his neck . . . there's sweat collecting in that crease on his head. [He indicates these as he describes them, using a *magic marker* on the back of Homer's head.] . . . And stress is collecting in the trouble spots here . . . here . . . and here . . . [Bart makes X marks on the back of Homer's head resembling eyes and a nose] making for one unhappy pappy."

Tying it all together is the music. "Bag Me a Homer" by Lurleen Lumpkin should have been on *Billboard*'s Top Twenty—with a bullet. Beverly D'Angelo is this sweet-talkin', country singin' guest star. She slays with all three songs she sings in this episode. Too bad we don't get to hear her other favorites, "I'm Bastin' a Turkey with My Tears," "Don't Look Up My Dress Unless You Mean It," and "I'm Sick of Your Lyin' Lips and False Teeth." Sing it, Lurleen.

Finally, to finish off the production end of the show, the actors go in one more time to do a final clean up of the voice track. This is then added to the composite music track and is assembled with the sound effects. And that's it! Four days later, we are all watching it in the comfort of our own homes in "Springfield," U.S.A., wherever that may be!

The Day the Music Died

► **THURSDAY, MAY 28, 1998**

*I**was in a trance; numb. I felt about as real as a cartoon. I was supposed** to be at* The Simpsons. *Instead, I found myself back home again, standing in my kitchen. I'm all right. I'm all right.*

It is our favorite gathering place. Everyone convenes in this cheeriest and warmest of places. The bright colors seem to pull in the satellites we have become, like a sun drawing in its children, its planets. Five minutes alone in this room would be an eternity. Someone, be it husband, children, assistant, housekeeper or dogs, is always right there beside me. But on this day, no one was anywhere to be found, except the dogs. The dogs were jumping all around me reminding me that I owe them some play time. I reached down and hugged Buddy, so soft, so skinny. He reminds me of Santa's Little Helper. Except he is jet-black.

I think it was Buddy. I'm not so sure. My hands didn't feel. But I did feel a warm tongue lick the tears from my cheeks.

The news came while I was on the way to the studio. I was on the 405 headed south. The traffic was the same as any Ride-Share Thursday. Don't quite know why Thursday is given the label. Seems to me every day on the 405 should be designated for a ride-share. I fill the time listening to books-on-tape so I don't mind the traffic. Side two of today's tape ended, so I flipped on the radio for a traffic update. I was near the Sepulveda Pass. Bad reception. I tuned around, ending on some acerbic FM station. This morning jock was in the middle of a comment that seemed even more odd than his daily dose of put-down. I am not a fan and I was reaching for the scan—"It's just so sad . . . terrible . . . loss . . . comedian . . . voice . . . television just won't be the same without him."

The words were disrupted by poor reception, which only made them more chilling. Somehow, coming from the font of discontent is a tone of sincerity I had never heard on a morning radio show. Someone . . . A shot of electricity went up my arms, to my neck and into my head. My hair stood on end. I slammed on the brakes! Inches from hitting the SUV in front of me. Damn! Too close! Who was he talking about? What happened? When did it happen? The reception came back suddenly but the deejay was gone and a commercial was hawking a hair-loss product. Dang! I flipped stations, anxiously trying to find another source. No such luck. Something inside me knew. Something inside me was telling me that it was not a joke. Damn radio! I surrendered and settled on a music station. Louis Armstrong, accompanied by Kenny G, came on singing *"What a Wonderful World."* Too weird. *Traffic released, responding to some mysterious elasticity, and it was smooth sailing to Fox.*

I pulled up and parked illegally, directly in front of Trailer 746. I was blocking some of NYPD Blue's *execs' cars. There must have been at least a dozen assorted Mercedeses, Beemers, Lexi and SUVs—all black—go figure. Normally, there might be a* Simpsons *writer out front taking a last puff, a lungful to get him through the forty-five minutes of table-read. But not today. Today, everyone was outside just milling around. Their faces were drawn and some were actually holding each other. Not a good sign. After ten years we are way beyond daily hugs. Did we get canceled? I wondered, knowing it was something much worse. Some of the writers, slumped, were huddled together, shaking their heads with that familiar look that says there is nothing to say. Others were heading off like dust motes, floating off to offices and cars, moving like odd powerless sticks in a strange way, devoid of hope. Tears wetted some cheeks. Others wore stiff faces on stiff spines, teeth grinding.*

I just sat there, the music winding down. My car just sat right in the middle of the road.

I noticed as I was getting out of the car that Mike Scully was coming my way. I asked him, "What happened?" He shook his head and told me that Phil had been shot to death.

I gasped, "Shot to death!? Omygod, how?"

Again, he shook his head. "His wife shot him and then shot herself."

My *jaw fell and let the air out of my knees. Mike was there. He reached out and hooked his arm through mine. I steadied myself on his shoulder.*

"Omygod. Omygod. Omygod. How could this have happened?" He didn't answer. I looked at him. He looked so small, like a lost boy. We sort of propped each other up for a moment. In all the years we had worked together this was the first time our relationship had touched on such a personal level. It was one of those unfortunate yet enlightening moments, an earthquake of the heart that brings out the heroic, the generous in us.

"Go on home," he managed to say. "We aren't going to do this today. Someone will call you." So I headed obediently home, not exactly sure if I was going to make it. Thank God all you have to do is hit the gas and steer in the right direction. I was a good little robot. I don't remember starting the car. I don't even remember turning it off. I didn't turn on the radio. I didn't listen to music. I didn't even pick up my cell phone. I didn't want to talk to anyone. I just drove, silently, shaking my head in that way that says there is nothing to say.

This "Kid" really misses her friend Phil.

"Be Still, My (Brave) Heart"

► NOVEMBER 12, 1998

We were called to an "afternoon" table-read today . . . normally it's at ten, so I knew something was up. Apparently, by juggling the reading schedule around, we could get our entire cast to the read and have our special guest there too; so great lengths were taken to pull this off. I had wanted to bring a friend and his kids to the show but Mike Scully held the line. "I'm sorry, Nancy. Someone, but we can't tell you who, is going to be there, so sorry, no extra guests." He wrote this episode and he was wearing his excitement on his sleeve. I pleaded my case, knowing what a soft touch Mike is if kids are involved. He gave in. "Yeah, it's okay, we'll make room."

We arrived—myself, my pal and two wide-eyed youth—to hustle 'n' bustle. This hadn't happened since Elizabeth Taylor's grand entrance. The room was well beyond SRO with the overflow leaning against the counter in the back. Word must have leaked out as to who was coming, even though I didn't know yet! Who are *these people? Welcome to another "Celeb Circus," I thought. Before I worked my way around the table, I jimmied my friends into a spot at the far end of the room. I nudged my way through the excited chatter and finally arrived at my seat. I wedged in.

Somehow, I was able to sit in my normal spot—funny how that happens. It isn't like we have been assigned seats or anything. It's just that after doing the show for about ten years, you tend to gravitate to the same seat week after week. You know how that is. Remember grade school? I don't know about you, but we always "claimed" our territory, whether it was around the campfire in scouts or at the table in the cafeteria. Well, Bart is in the fourth grade, you know. That's my excuse, at any rate. So week after week, year after year, I park my buns in the same chair, unless another set of seat cushions who doesn't know the de facto seating arrangement beats me to it.

As the room filled up even more, the only chair that remained unoccupied was the one right next to mine. Not hard to figure that this was the designated hot seat for today's Mystery Guest. The new kid in town would be sitting there. I hoped he was cool, cute even, just like when Peter Chennie sat next to me in Miss Harrington's fourth grade class. Yummmyyyy.

We chatted away about dis 'n' dat and signed a stack of autograph requests. There was some speculation about who's the *mystery guest gonna be; we were all enjoying the surprise, the break in the routine, the arrival of a new kid in class; but it was really just another day at our great gig. We were a team, the hot-doggers on the playground, ready to play another round of Spring-field, the game of voice-activated kickball.*

A hush fell over the room and I looked up, knowing the mystery guest, the new kid, had arrived, and who should stand in the doorway but none other than Mel Gibson! Omygod, he is even more gorgeous in person! You just can't not notice those striking baby blues. They were sharp and bright as he scanned the room to find someone in charge. He was dressed very casually—alas, no kilt, 'tis a pity. He wore a comfortable shirt, a baseball cap and very tight jeans. Didn't notice what were on his feet. My eyes roamed the regions from his quads on up. Up, up and up from the delicious south to the extreme north. Easy, girl, easy! My mind whiffed his hair and imagined the smell of some fresh organic shampoo . . . Suddenly my nasopharynx was getting turned on, in spite of the fact that there were doughnuts, bagels, fruit and coffee between us. Perhaps his shampoo is imported from his homeland, Down Under, I thought. The thought of "Down Under" got my eyes drifting south again. Man of the Year? I should say so! What a total Babe Magnet.

Mel must have sensed everyone looking at him because he was very reserved. Bonnie stepped forward, cool as can be, and introduced him to Matt and to Mike and then began to escort him to his seat. Oh, yeah! They walked around the end of the table, passing Harry, Julie, Karl, Hank, Pamela, Maggie, Marcia,

Yeardley, Tress, Dan, and finally the new kid sat right next to
moi! Just lucky, I guess.

See, the only time I had experienced this was with Petie, the
absolutely cutest boy in all the school. He too had been the "new
kid" and the moment I set eyes on him, he was mine! He was
from somewhere exotic, like Colorado, or . . . Colombia. You can
imagine my delight when he was escorted into the room and introduced to our class. My little ten-year-old heart went pit-a-pat
and suddenly I knew what Valentine's Day was all about. There
was an empty desk beside mine. Please, oh, please, let him sit here!
I screamed internally. I didn't just have a crush on him, I had a
whole train wreck of emotions that were somehow being revital-
ized as Mel wedged his very tight buns in the seat next to me. (Did
I mention how tight his buns are?) I was the lucky one again! I
get to sit next to Pet . . . er, Mel! I could now smell that shampoo
. . . and I could imagine, on this first, nervous day of "school,"
what it must feel like to be in Mel's pants—oops, excuse me, I
mean shoes . . . Mel's shoes!

I am sure that Mel was very aware of the effect he was creating in that room, right then and there. He was getting his script
ready to read, his head was bowed down and a very fine layer of
sweat started to bead up on his upper lip. You can't help but notice
things like his eyes, hair, lips . . . mmmm. Too shy to say anything,
I watched out of the corner of my eye as he wiped a drop of sweat
from his sideburn and readjusted his baseball cap.

Peter Chennie had had that same little layer of sweat, the
little guy. He also wore a baseball cap and kept taking it off and
twisting it in his hands, then putting it back on again. I remem-

ber Miss Harrington introducing him to the rest of the class. Petie kept his curly head bowed and barely looked at anyone. I felt for him. Right then, he had won my heart. He seemed like such a scared little boy, but you don't dare show that in the fourth grade!

The episode, "Beyond Blunderdome," is a satirical exposé of what it might be like to be a movie star in Hollywood. What better casting than the Sexiest Man in the Universe? I wonder if Tom Cruise, George Clooney or Brad Pitt lost the part to Mel?

As we got into the read, it didn't matter who read a good line—whenever there was a laugh in the room, all eyes went to Mel. "Is he laughing? Does Mel think it's funny?" It is hard enough being a guest on a show that has been around for so long, but being a celebrity guest is just like being that new kid in the fourth grade. There is a ritual, a silent hazing ceremony that each goes through and today was Mel's turn. We knew he had done John Smith in Pocahontas, but, hey, that's not The Simpsons! This is our classroom, our playground, and the new kid, no matter what reputation he made in that other school, still has to kick the ball. So, two hundred eyeballs were locked on Mel, watching him step into the kicker's box. I was beginning to feel the enormous size of Mel's shoes and was glad they were on his feet and not mine!

His first line was fast approaching. He was about to become a member of the elite club of guests who have been willing to poke fun at themselves. We love them! But would he measure up? Would all that on-screen talent translate into our world of 'toons? His first words came and went, sounded good.

WILLIAM
(A Studio Exec):

(REASSURING) Relax, Mel. Everyone's going to love it.

MEL:

Really? You're not just saying that because I'm number ten in Entertainment Weekly's *Power 100?*

ROBYN
(Another Exec):
I thought you were number twenty.
(Mel shoots her a look.)

The captive audience ate it up. Mel was doing fine but it was all pretty easy so far, nothing too hard to kick around the yard. But a test was fast approaching.

At one point in the script, there was the direction: "Curly laugh." Mel leaned over, pointing out the direction in the script, and whispered, his scent sending shivers up and down my spine, "Hey, Hi. What's a 'Curly laugh'?"

I had heard that he was a real practical joker and I figured this was just a setup but, like a true "crushed" ten-year-old, I just whispered, "You know, 'Ynuck! Ynuck! Ynuck!'" Mel's eyes lit up even more, if such a thing is possible, and, just as he heard his cue, he let out this perfectly timed and brilliantly executed rendition of that signature laugh from The Three Stooges. *Everyone busted a gut. He had kicked the ball out of the yard! Suddenly the* distance between Mel and the rest of us became smaller. *The new kid from the big school, with all his credits, awards, recognition and paparazzi, was now officially one of* The Simpsons.

The reading ended with applause and cheers for our guest. As he stood to leave he was swamped by awestruck kudos. I desperately tried to keep my eyes from drifting too obviously toward those jeans, but I held my ground, enjoying the fact that I was still beside him, basking in the overflow of aura directed at the new kid. The crowd thinned a bit and my guests made their way to me. "That was great, Nance. Thanks." My friend's kids were at sea. I tried to explain what a rarity it is to have our guest star actually work with us, when I felt a shift behind me and turned to see Mel take a step toward the door. I didn't know what to say. My heart was in my throat. I didn't feel I could speak. Suddenly I felt the same way I had felt when the bell rang for recess: Petie ran out and left me standing in Miss Harrington's classroom all alone. I just wanted to tell him that I was glad he was in our class.

I reached for my purse and my script and as I started to leave, Mel turned back to me, taking a moment out of the sea of "Thanks" and "Good work, Mels." He turned to me with a wink. "I owe you one, Curly."

Oh, yeah!

The Celebrity of Bart

"So what," do you ask, "is it like to be the voice behind the star?" "How does it make you feel to know that the real celebrities of the show are hand-drawn characters?" "Is it true that when you first started doing the show the producers didn't want you talking about doing the voices because they wanted to keep it a secret?"

It is quite a curiosity being a celebrity that nobody knows. I ask you, How many stars would you *not* recognize were they to walk down the street? Sure they can disguise themselves with wigs, hats, sunglasses, but how many of them can literally go anywhere dressed in everyday normal clothes and not be mobbed or at least gawked at by the public? I can think of no one—besides my fellow cast members and me. The anonymity factor is such a unique aspect of this job. I must admit, sometimes I wish it were different.

I was asked to be a presenter for a special tribute to animation at the Screen Actors Guild Awards on March 7, 1999. This was unprecedented. Never before had the voices behind animation been acknowledged publicly. I was so thrilled and so honored to have been asked. The idea was that I would be introduced and walk onstage to the down-center spot. I would introduce a film clip of some of the top voice-over talent in the industry and also include some celebrities who have created memorable characters. It was another highlight of my career.

I went to a rehearsal and must have gone up and down those steps about a dozen times. They are not normal-sized steps and I didn't want to be looking at my feet while going down them. The last thing I wanted to do was "make a splash" right in front of Tom Hanks, Cate Blanchett, Robert Duvall and Kathy Bates—not to mention the other 150 or so nominees! I had memorized my speech so I could have complete eye contact with the audience—this was one of the times that I didn't want to rely on the script or TelePrompTer to feed me my lines. This was, after all, live and in-person!

I was so nervous—*excited* nervous. The audience was filled with celebrities, celebrities whose identities are associated with the last project they did on film or television. I find it interesting how much perception has to do with visual cues. And there I was, a celebrity that nobody knew.

There were some questions about how I would be introduced and what I was going to say until I told the producer that he just had to trust me on this one. I had done dozens of public appearances by then and there was no doubt in mind. So we came to an agreement and I learned my part.

The moment finally arrived. I was introduced and with the grace of a model but the suppressed enthusiasm of a girl on prom night made my entrance down the nine steps. I hit my mark and giving the audience the once over until I got everyone's full attention, I said, "I'm Bart Simpson. Who the hell are you?" and it brought the house down! It was utterly wonderful. All the nervous energy in the room subsided, if only temporarily, when the words came from my mouth. It was the perfect opening line, especially for this elite group anxiously awaiting the announcement of their categories.

The only odd thing about the evening was when I first arrived. I had been picked up in a limo and the crowd, the paparazzi and all the reporters and their crews were packed in front of the Shrine Auditorium. Cameras were popping; the crowd was chanting, "Julia! Julia! Julia!" because Julia Roberts had just arrived with nominee-boyfriend Benjamin Bratt. Of course, right in front of them were Angelina Jolie, Jimmy Smits and Gwyneth Paltrow. It was a pretty star-studded night.

I was escorted over to where the announcer was located to let him know that I had arrived. He announces new arrivals to the crowd so they can basically scream their heads off, trying to get the celebrity's attention. It is all very good for publicity and a fun evening for some of the truly dedicated fans. The only thing was, he never said my name. He was told again that I had arrived and still didn't say my name. Then he was told that I was there to present a special award for animation, but no go. Finally, duh, I realized that he wasn't going to say my name, not now, not ever. Never. So I went ahead and walked the red-carpeted walk, and no one knew who I was. I passed behind Calista Flockhart and Brooke Shields. The crowd was immersed in the thrill of seeing their most favorite stars from the shows they love and videotape and I must admit that that was a very odd feeling. But it isn't always that way.

It was quite a different story when I went to kick off an art exhibition at the Animation Art Gallery in London. The gallery is located on Great Castle Street and gets a lot of walk-in traffic. The owners of the gallery, Graham Parker and Russell Singler, had invited me to be a special guest and this was an opportunity I couldn't resist. I had heard how London, and most of Europe for that matter, was totally crazy for *The Simpsons*. I just had to see for myself.

I spent most of the week doing tons of promotion. I was on *The Big Breakfast*, which has a fast-paced morning news/entertainment format. It has the feel of a game show and a stand-up comedy routine—nothing quite like it in America. I was also a guest on *Blue Peter*, which is the longest running children's show on television in the United Kingdom. It is well organized and runs like clockwork. The staff of the show were truly fascinated with the idea that Bart was a woman. I gave out a bunch of autographs and, in return, I got a really cool pin that, no matter where

I wore it, everyone wanted! Apparently, owning a *Blue Peter* pin means that you have joined the ranks of ambassador or perhaps noble lord in that country.

But the most memorable, if not embarrassing moment was when I appeared on *The Chris Evans Show*. He shoots his show live at the Riverside Studios, Hammersmith. The audience is standing on the stage while Chris is located upstairs in a room that they converted into the set. The cameras are suspended on wires and go sailing through the air. I am given my cue on the catwalk high above everyone below. Lining the walk are tons of fans and on-camera it creates a wonderful perspective. I felt like such a star! It was a bit overwhelming. The show began and I heard my name. I started to make my entrance and by the time I arrived where Chris was sitting, he was up on his feet and hugging me. Then, instead of sitting down to interview me, he joined the masses of people in the audience and started bowing as if I were a goddess! He was down on his knees! I couldn't believe it. He kept bowing and bowing and everyone was just eating it up. Then he started to take his seat opposite me, but the crowd was still going nuts, so he was up again, in the audience and down on his knees. This is what I live for—all men should bow to women, er . . . uh, Bart . . . uh, me!

Anyone who is anyone knows that when Chris Evans likes something, he lets you know it. And when he doesn't—he lets you know that too. I am just glad that he has to be one of the all-time biggest fans of the show! He was doing everything he could to make me feel comfortable. All was going well when he asked me, "Did you have any idea that the show was going to be as big a hit as it is?" to which I replied, "I had sort of thought that the show would be successful, but I had no idea that nearly ten years later I would be sitting across the desk of the most popular show in the United Kingdom, opposite Chris *Owans*!" And everyone just howled. I had no idea why everyone thought that was so funny. Chris looked straight at the audience and without dropping a beat said, "Chris Owans, eh?" And I still did not realize my faux pas. "*The Chris Owans Show,* eh?!" Omygod was I embarrassed! Nothing like a good dose of humble-pie to straighten out my ego, which was rapidly approaching megastar proportions.

After five full days of promoting, the opening day of the exhibition finally arrived. Graham and Russell had organized everything so beautifully. We had had an invite-only reception the night before and although there were quite a few people there, it was nothing like the *2,000* that waited in the queue *for three hours* to meet me the next day! It was unbelievable. I was seated on a couch in a special sectioned-off space. The security guard kept the crowd at bay, while they were individually ushered in to see me. There were so many people, I just had enough time to have them come sit beside me for a fifteen-second chat, then off they went. It was extraordinary. I worked fairly nonstop for three hours—hi, bye ... hi, bye ... hi, bye—and on and on. Now I know how Santa feels.

There was a similar reaction in Melbourne, Australia, when I flew in to visit Andrew VanEmbden and Danny Samuels at the Comic Art Gallery in Armadale. I was treated like royalty. The oddest thing was that I had contracted laryngitis and never did recover my voice the whole time I was there. But the boys made sure that I had everything I needed and my good friend, confidante and escort, Carmella Scoggins from the Fox Animation Archives, made sure that I wasn't overworked and underfed. (The latter is never a problem.)

I had said earlier that the SAG Awards set an unprecedented example by publicly acknowledging the voice-over industry. This is actually a half-truth. Back in August 1992, Dan, Julie, Yeardley, Marcia Wallace, Jackie Mason and I were awarded special Emmys for "Outstanding Voice-Over Performance." This was a special juried award from the Board of Governors. There was not a category at the time in which we could be acknowledged because, quite frankly, there wasn't any competition. I couldn't believe that we were actually receiving Emmys! There are just an outrageous number of categories, so there just isn't enough time to air every single award winner. To solve this problem, the ceremony was held the night before and we were mentioned the next evening during the televised version. I have to admit I was totally bummed that we weren't going to partake in the televised version, however it was still quite a remarkable honor. I took that Emmy and ran!

Without a doubt, the highlight of my career was when the whole lot of us were in Aspen, in February 2000, at the U.S. Comedy Arts Festival. It was the first time I felt we were publicly acknowledged as an ensemble, and that made a world of difference. The Festival and HBO were the hosts of the event. The previous year the whole group from *Monty Python* received the honor. But this was the first year that the recipient was also invited to perform. Yes, that's right—we were invited to perform two staged readings of our scripts *live!* It isn't like doing a live reading is any big deal—after all, we've done over 250 of them in the past eleven years!—except that this was in front of a standing-room-only audience who had packed themselves into the Wheeler Opera House! We are used to doing the reading for a modest hundred or so. The Wheeler Opera House holds *five hundred!* How cool is that?

I decided that I was going to be a star for this event. I brought only one jacket, my *Simpsons* jacket. I figured that this has happened so few times in my career that I just wanted to milk it for all it was worth. I don't know that I will ever do that again, but I am so glad I did. Everywhere I went, people would whisper, "There she is. There's Bart" or "There's Nancy Cartwright, the voice of Bart Simpson." My sisters had joined me and one of them was absolutely stunned about the reaction. She was concerned that my whole life would never be my own—that now everyone was going to be invading my personal space and I would never have any privacy. But I knew that this was one small town and this was one remarkable event. I didn't know if we would ever have this opportunity again, so I reassured her. I let her know that once I got on that airplane and headed home, I would just be Nancy Cartwright. My short, female and blond identity would disguise my alterego, ten-year-old Bart, and no one would know any better. And that is exactly what happened. It truly is the best of both worlds.

We had all been flown in and put up at the St. Regis, the ritziest hotel in town. First class all the way. Even in the transfer in Denver, a representative from the Festival was awaiting our arrival to escort us to the next terminal. Thank God for that. If you have ever had to transfer to a flight in Denver, you know what I mean. (We got to ride in one of those oversized golf carts—cool, man—"Beep, beep. Comin' through!")

Once we arrived and were all settled in, we had a rehearsal. Excitement was in the air. I don't believe I have ever felt this kind of unity with the group since ... I don't know when. It was astounding and truly the beginning of more good times while in Aspen.

The first show was at six-thirty the next evening. We gathered in the greenroom with assorted drinks, nibbles and snacks and then were routed backstage so the show could begin. The evening started with a ten-minute clip of some of the favorite scenes of the show. It was really fun sitting backstage and listening to the audience let out gasps of recognition as a new clip was shown. This select group of dedicated fans was absolutely loving it! Some of the clips actually got applause and, by the end, they could hardly wait for the live portion of the show to begin. Matt Groening kicked everything off with a couple of quips and then introduced Mike Scully, who introduced the actors. One by one we paraded in and took our seats onstage.

The backdrop was very simple and yet elegant—huge, oversized picture frames with drapes of gold cloth lit in rich hues of purples, blues and magentas. Stunning. We were all dressed in "Aspen-hip," which is very close to "L.A.-hip," plus snow. The audience went wild! They were pumped and we were primed. It was history in the making.

The first script we read was "Homer's Enemy." Normally, back in L.A. we get plenty of laughs among ourselves. We are, I thought, our best audience. *Wrong!* This night could not be beat.

With each new character "making an entrance" the audience ooh'd and aaaah'd and sometimes even stopped the show for a second with a smattering of applause.

They just couldn't be more pleased. And when the act breaks occurred, they even applauded then. Amazing. When we finished, they were up on their feet for a standing O!

We settled back onto our stools and then the audience had a chance to ask us some questions. What was really cool was that no one had any. All they wanted to hear was more of the voices! "Do Krusty!" "What would Apu say?" "Who does Mrs. Skinner?" It was absolutely extraordinary. This group truly did not have any questions! They were so dedicated that they already knew every answer anyway, but more than that, just wanted to see the actor and hear the voice together!

Our next show, as if it could get any better, was the next night at 11:30 P.M. Quite a different crowd simply because of the late-night hour. We did a totally different script—lucky for the guy who actually snagged tickets for both events! "Lisa's Date with Density" did not disappoint. Again, an SRO crowd, they were packed in like patrons at Moe's during Happy Hour. The only difference on that evening was that the word was out and 300 very disappointed people did not get into the show. Can you dig it? The cops had to be called because this actually caused a bit of a riot! Didn't think it could get cooler.

But the best moment for me was when I was onstage that first night, Yeardley to my left and Dan to my right, and 500 of Springfield's finest were captivated, holding on to our every word. At one moment, someone said something and the crowd loved it. Then it happened again and again. The laughter was consistent and contagious. Everyone loved it! But over the merriment, one laugh stood out. I heard it once, I heard it twice. It was a sound that was very familiar to me.

Just a week prior to the trip, I lay in bed at three in the morning not able to sleep. I clicked on "Nick at Nite" to catch an old *Mary Tyler Moore* episode. If you watch that show and listen very carefully, you too will hear what I heard. There is one laugh that stands out, head and shoulders above any other laugh in that audience. You can't miss it. It is distinctive. It is warm. It is vital. And it is incredibly validative. I wondered what it would be like to be Mary Tyler Moore, or Ed Asner or Ted Knight or Gavin MacLeod or Valerie Harper. I wondered what it would be like to be standing on the set of that show in front of a live audience, taping the episode and hearing *that* laugh. Well, I found out one week later, sitting on the stage in front of a live audience doing the reading when that familiar sound rang out. It was undeniable. It is the single, most validating sound any artist can hear. It is the sound of pure pleasure. That is what I feel every time I hear Jim Brooks laugh . . . even to this day. The greatest moment in my history of *The Simpsons* was when Jim Brooks laughed with such abandon the opening night of the Aspen Festival. He is my hero.

Bart's celebrity status really makes me recognize the power and responsibility that goes with the territory. Once I was called by the Make-A-Wish Foundation. A young man, age thirteen or so, was dying of cancer and his wish was to fly to Hollywood and have lunch with Bart Simpson and also to tour Universal Studios.

I was really touched and it would be one of my greatest joys to be able to fulfill this young man's wish.

About a week before he was to fly out, I got a call from the foundation. I was told that the young man was not going to be able to make the flight after all. The air-pressure changes on the flight were too extreme for his body and his doctor denied him permission. "Well," I said to the rep, "if he can't come to me, I'll just go to him." If there was some way that I could make his fading life just a little bit better, then that was what I had to do. So I flew to his home and spent the next several hours talking to him and his immediate family.

It is hard to describe what I felt. Here was this beautiful family—mother, father, little sister. They had gone through months and months of medical assistance, chemotherapy, radiation, counseling, etc. And here I am, brand-new on the scene, not knowing these people and seeing this kid for the first time. This was one of the most difficult and painful experiences to go through, but it was just a touch of what his family must have been experiencing. The boy couldn't talk, as he was all wired up and tubes were everywhere. But his eyes sparkled as I told one story after another to him and his family. They all had questions and I just ended up doing lots of voices and answering every question they had.

After a while, he was a little tired and it was time for me to go. I left the little sister as many posters and autographed items as I had left the young man. It hurt to be there, but the joy I felt, knowing that I had given this young man pleasure, made it all worth the trip.

Later, I found out that he had recovered just enough to actually make that flight to Universal Studios. He got to take the tour after all. Then, that night, back at the hotel, the little guy passed away. Bless his heart. He did it. He got his wish.

I have been involved with a nonprofit organization called Famous Fone Friends for about ten years now. The purpose is to bring a little cheer to kids who are diagnosed with cancer or who have been in a life-debilitating accident by calling them on the phone. There are many celebrities, including on-camera actors like Ben Savage, David Hasselhoff, Rosie O'Donnell and Jay Leno who are also quite active in this. As popular as their live-action shows might be, this is a perfect venue for voice-over artists, as you can imagine, because it is all done by telephone. Can you imagine being eight years old and receiving a call from Captain Hook, Roger Rabbit, Pinky or Phil and/or Lil? Well, Corey Burton, Jess Harnell, Rob Paulsen and Kath Souci are a few of the unsung voice-over artists who dedicate time regularly, calling kids who need a little brightness in their lives.

I remember one time calling a little guy who was recovering from surgery. I spoke to his mother first. She told me that he was very excited I was on the phone but that he couldn't talk and would that be all right? I told her it was fine, so she put him on. We proceeded to have a "conversation" that lasted for about five minutes. I just kept talking and assuming that he was getting everything that I said. I actually felt like I was communicating with him telepathically more than telephonically—it was pretty wild. At the end of the conversation, his mother got back on the line and said that his face was a bright red and he was so happy and excited but that he was going to need a little oxygen so we were going to have to stop! Oops, didn't mean to do that.

My fans mean everything to me. I get tons of fan mail and respond to each letter. My offices are set up with a whole postal station that enables me to read, sign, stuff, lick and stamp all the requests I get from fans all over the world. I have been doing this since the beginning of the show and love doing this for kids, and the parents who disguise themselves as kids! At first I only responded to the letters addressed to me personally, but soon the letters to Bart were routed to me and I respond to them too. It is now just a part of my daily routine. Kids will write some of the funniest things and some pretty emotional letters too.

I got one letter from a fan that reads, "This summer I am hosting a girl from Northern Ireland and she is so excited about everything here. She told me back home in Belfast whenever *The Simpsons* comes on, no one talks on the phone but stays glued to their TVs. They really love the show and it is a common ground between the Catholics and the Protestants. It really is amazing that with all the troubles there with religion that a cartoon can give people something in common."

Just before graduating from high school, I auditioned in front of my classmates to be selected to do a commencement speech. There were about a dozen of us who had written our own speeches and this was a great honor. I wrote a speech about how our actions, no matter how big or small, can influence those around us. It pretty much summarized my belief in the power of art and aesthetics, something I still believe in today. My speech was inspired by this poem by Henry Wadsworth Longfellow:

Lives of great men remind us
We can make our lives sublime.
And in departing, leave behind us
Footprints on the sands of Time.

Halfway into the speech, I lost my place. My mind went blank and the words no longer came out of my mouth. But I stood there, very poised, and just took a moment to look at the audience. I carefully looked at my classmates and, within moments, the words came back and I picked right up where I had left off, not dropping one thought.

Later that afternoon, the selectees were announced over the P.A. I did not get chosen. I was devastated. I told my mom and she gave me a big hug and said that someday I would have another opportunity to influence people. She told me that people will always judge and criticize, but as long as I remained honest and true, no one could take that away from me. Mom was right again.

Bart Simpson and *The Simpsons* have left an indelible footprint on the history of television, if not our culture altogether. And I am so proud to be a part of it, and I thank *you*.

Appendix

Some celebrities have stayed after their first appearance on the show, or come back for regular visits. Albert Brooks has visited Springfield four separate times as four different characters: Bob, the operator of Bob's RV Roundup; Jacques, Marge's bowling instructor; Brad Goodman, a soft-spoken self-help guru; and Hank Scorpio, the President of Globex Corporation. Jon Lovitz has visited Springfield three times, as Professor Lombardo, the art professor at Springfield Community College; Aristotle Amadopolis, the owner/operator of the Shelbyville Nuclear Power Plant; and Llewellyn Sinclair, the director of various Springfield theatrical productions. And finally, making more guest appearances than anyone else, Phil Hartman as Smooth Jimmy Apollo, a professional football prognosticator on TV; Lyle Lanley, a fast-talking salesman/con man; Evan Conover, the undersecretary of state for International Protocol, Brat and Punk Division;

and the ever-persistent Troy McClure, a onetime B-movie idol and present host of all infomercials, funerals, award shows, telethons, do-it-yourself videos, TV specials and educational films relating to Springfield.

Then there are those who created one extraordinarily memorable character. Ron Taylor broke our hearts with Bleeding Gums Murphy. Looking back through my scripts—(you didn't think I'd throw *them* away, did you?! And, again, no, you can't get copies!)—I realized that Ron had only been our guest star twice. But somehow, with all the energy and passion, pathos and heart he put in Bleeding Gums' soul, I could have sworn he must have visited Springfield at least twenty times! Harvey Fierstein only brought his carry-on luggage while he visited Springfield for one afternoon, but his rendition of Karl, Homer's personal assistant, showed some truth and made all of us want him to come visit more often. And Kelsey Grammer scores big-time by injecting caustic, bitter, contemptuous and deliciously vile energy into his rendition of Sideshow Bob. Springfield just wouldn't be the same without him.

Other memorable characters include: Cloris Leachman as Mrs. Glick, an elderly acquaintance of Marge; Danny DeVito as Homer's long-lost brother; Doris Grau as Lunchlady Doris; Alex Rocco as Roger Meyers, Jr.—the founder of Itchy & Scratchy International and disputed creator of the Itchy & Scratchy cartoon characters; Kathleen Turner as Stacy Lovell, the inventor of the Malibu Stacy doll; Ted Danson, Woody Harrelson, Rhea Perlman, John Ratzenberger and George Wendt playing their *Cheers* characters; Joe Mantegna as Fat Tony; Joan Kenley (the official AT&T voice) as the phone voice; Harry Morgan as Bill Gannon; Tom Poston as the Capital City's mascot, Goofball; George Takei as Akira, the waiter at the Happy Sumo Japanese restaurant; Tracey Ullman as Emily Winthrop, the owner/operator of Emily Winthrop's Canine College; Audrey Meadows as Bea, a resident of the Springfield Retirement Castle; Dustin Hoffman (Sam Etic) as Mr. Bergstrom, Lisa's substitute teacher; Michael Jackson (John Jay Smith) as Leon Kompowsky, a 300-pound mental patient; Jackie Mason as Rabbi Krustofski, for which role he received an Emmy; Beverly D'Angelo as Lurleen Lumpkin, a cocktail waitress at the Beer 'N' Brawl; Sara Gilbert as Laura Powers, a pubescent heartthrob baby-sitter; Michelle Pfeiffer as Mindy Simmons, a Springfield Nuclear Power Plant engineer/temptress; Sam Neill as Molloy, a cat burglar; Winona Ryder as Allison, a seven-year-old gifted new student; Meryl Streep as Jessica Lovejoy, the discreetly incorrigible only daughter of Helen and the Rev.; Anne Bancroft as Dr. Zweig, a Springfield psychoanalyst; Patrick Stewart as Number One, the head of the Stonecutters; Susan Sarandon as the Springfield Elementary ballet teacher; Mandy Patinkin as Hugh Parkfield, a brilliant student, suave individual and humorless vegetarian; Glenn Close as Mother Simpson; R. Lee Ermey as Col. Leslie "Hap" Hapablap, a colonel in the U.S. Air Force; Matt Groening as Matt Groening, the gun-toting creator of *The Simpsons* and comics such as "Damnation," "Johnny Reb" and "True Murder Stories"; Lawrence Tierney as Det. Don Brodka, the head of security at the Tri-N-Save Store; Donald Sutherland as Hollis Hurlbut, the president of the Springfield

Historical Society; Kirk Douglas as Chester J. Lampwick, a bum in Bumtown (the bad part of Springfield); Christina Ricci as Erin, a somewhat inarticulate youth; Rodney Dangerfield as Larry Burns, a souvenir hawker; Johnny Cash as Coyote, a coyote; Gillian Anderson and David Duchovny as Scully and Mulder; Jack Lemmon as Frank Ormand, the pretzel man; Maggie Roswell as Shary Bobbins, the magical nanny of British ancestry, not to be confused with Mary Poppins; John Waters as John, the owner/operator of Cockamamie's collectible shop; David Hyde Pierce as Cecil, Springfield's Chief Hydrological and Hydrodynamical engineer/diabolical embezzler; Dave Thomas as Rex Banner, a lawman sent from Washington to clean up Springfield's bootlegging during modern-day prohibition; Sab Shimono as Mr. Sparkle, a cleaning detergent that is a magnet for foodstuffs; Willem Dafoe as Commandant, the head honcho at the Rammelwood Military Academy; Martin Sheen as the real Sgt. Seymour Skinner, an American who was sold to China for slave labor and forced to make sneakers at gunpoint in Wuhan; Andrea Martin as Apu's mother; Helen Hunt as Renee, a professional flower vendor; Rod Steiger as Captain Tenille, a man of few words; Steve Martin as Ray Patterson, a former sanitation commissioner; Brendan Fraser as Brad, a powersource huckster supreme; Steve Weber as Neil, just another huckster; Lisa Kudrow as Alex Whitney, a Calvin Klein pretension; Martin Mull as Seth, a hippie; George Carlin as Munchie, a little hippier; Mark Hamill as Leavelle, a professional bodyguard trainer; Fred Willard as Wally Kogen, a self-deprecating, yet loathsome former acquaintance of Homer's; Jan Hooks as Manjula, Apu's wife and mother of octuplets; and last but not least, Isabella Rossellini as Astrid Weller, the owner of the Louvre: American Style gallery. I wrote that all in one breath and I now am going for my transfusion.

(Long pause.)

Epilogue

While performing *In Search of Fellini* in 1995, my career focus began to shift. I realized, "Hey, *The Simpsons* is not going to be producing new shows forever! Someday, maybe soon, you might be saying, 'I *used* to be the voice of Bart Simpson.' "

So . . . never one to depend on fate, I established Happy House Productions, developing and producing projects for film, television and most currently, the internet. In order to promote the company, I founded a bimonthly newsletter, *The Nancy News*, that started out with a circulation of 300 and has grown to nearly 10,000. In keeping with the times, Happy House is also launching a destination Web site for animation and sports lovers, www.sportsanimation.com. Loaded with games and contests, it is the place to be! And for that personal touch, fans can always check out www.thenancyshow.com.

I *can* say "no," but I love being involved with the

greater community of mankind. I'm a member of the nonprofit International Animated Film Society, aka ASIFA. We encourage and support animation projects and artists throughout the world. Ironically, it was the opening night of my play that I garnered their highest honor given in the excellence of voice-overs, the prestigious Annie Award. (It sits next to my son's soccer and jog-a-thon trophies.)

I was recently elected to the Board of Directors of Women in Animation. We are immersed in the preservation and promotion of animated projects. I am also a founding member of the Chouinard Foundation, a nonprofit organization whose mission is dedicated to preserving and expanding the legacy of Nelbert Chouinard, a lifetime ally of Walt Disney.

It is through these organizations that we forward the rehabilitation of the artist in order to make it a better world. It is our passion to encourage young people to pursue their dreams, for it is only in this kind of focus that one will find fulfillment.

Active as a volunteer in my community, I also support good samaritan Linda Stone's Famous Fone Friends, bringing cheer on the phone to children and young adults who are terminally ill; big-hearted Neil Willenson's Camp Heartland, assisting children and young folks who are diagnosed as HIV-positive; philanthropy-driven Free Arts for Abused Children, bringing arts and crafts to children whose parents have abused them; and the following organizations that utilize the research of humanitarian L. Ron Hubbard: Narconon—a drug rehab program; The Way to Happiness—a guide to happy living; and The World Literacy Crusade—assisting those who have trouble learning. By allowing some time in my life to give to others who could use some encouragement, guidance and just a friendly call, I find a very good balance in my otherwise dull and listless life.

As animation has evolved over the years, hopefully so have I. I have been blessed with the opportunity to work on one of the greatest shows in the history of television. I get to work with wonderful people and have made some lifetime friends.

Writing this book came at just the right time. The challenges that it presented were numerous, but the joys of reflection offset the long hours and the pain of writer's cramp.

To you, good reader, may you enjoy many more hours of *The Simpsons*. There won't be anything like it again.